Pimple, Pranks & Pratfalls

The British Silent Cinema Group was formed in 1998 to promote research into British cinema before 1930, to facilitate the archiving of the national cinema from that period, and to sponsor the screening of British silent cinema to a wider audience. Each year, an extended weekend of screenings, papers and discussions is held at Broadway Media Centre in Nottingham, a collaboration between the British Film Institute, the National Film and Television Archive and the Broadway Cinema. Following the second weekend in 1999, devoted to silent British film comedy, it was decided to record the proceedings of each themed weekend in an annual publication, and thus make available the activities of the group to the widest possible public.

The work of the British Silent Cinema Group is overseen and coordinated by the following:

Laraine Porter, Broadway Media Centre
Bryony Dixon, National Film and Television Archive
Alan Burton, De Montfort University
Luke McKernan, British Universities Film and Video Council
Elaine Burrows, National Film and Television Archive
Frank Gray, South East Film and Video Archive
Christine Gledhill, Staffordshire University
John Hawkridge, University of Derby
Mike Hammond, University of Southampton
Paul Marygold, independent adviser

Pimple, Pranks & Pratfalls

British Film Comedy Before 1930

Edited by

Alan Burton and Laraine Porter

FLICKS
BOOKS

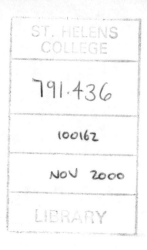
A CIP catalogue record for this book is available from the British Library.

ISBN 1 86236 010 3

First published in 2000 by

Flicks Books
29 Bradford Road
Trowbridge
Wiltshire BA14 9AN
England
Tel   +44 1225 767728
Fax   +44 1225 760418
Email   flicks.books@dial.pipex.com

Printed and bound in Great Britain by Antony Rowe Ltd

Contents

Introduction

Alan Burton and Laraine Porter

Over the past two decades, some of the most important interventions and developments in cinema studies have sprung from research into early and silent cinema. Each year, Le Giornate del Cinema Muto (Pordenone Silent Film Festival) brings together influential film theorists and historians from around the world with the latest discoveries, restorations and programmes from international film archives eliciting new insights and research into the history of world cinema. So it was that the idea of hosting a British silent cinema event with an associated publication was born. Long since eclipsed by its American counterpart, British early and silent cinema has had relatively low status among the world's scholars, despite the massive volume of material held in the National Film and Television Archive (NFTVA) and the opportunities for research this offers. The NFTVA is one of the largest and most accessible archives in the world, and the annual British Silent Cinema Weekend and this publication are a modest attempt to promote further research and exhibition projects which make use of these holdings.

Whether or not a piece of film comedy is intrinsically funny is highly subjective. None of the contributors in this volume would argue for the overall superiority of British silent film comedy compared to that produced in the United States, but all agree that its neglect is undeserved.

Both Bryony Dixon and Luke McKernan, respectively archivist and former cataloguer at the NFTVA, discuss the broad issues surrounding the national collection of British silent comedy, including possible reasons for its suppression among scholars, the broad themes and tendencies it exhibits, and the contexts into which it might be placed. McKernan offers insight into dominant comedic structures such as the chase and the miscreant clown figure, and discusses these within a socioeconomic framework, whereas Dixon addresses the origins of British comedy *vis-à-vis* the music-hall and theatre, and draws comparisons with American counterparts such as Charlie Chaplin and Stan Laurel whose antecedents were indeed on the British stage. Both archivists lament the neglect of British silent cinema and the resulting paucity of extant material, an issue echoed by Tony Fletcher, whose essay summarises quantitative research conducted by himself and others. Fletcher provides a useful overview of personalities and film titles, many of which have vanished into obscurity, and he offers a tantalising glimpse of the sheer volume of popular comedy produced during the silent period.

Early film pioneers are the subject of essays by Barry Anthony, Frank Gray and Garrett Monaghan. The prolific, if largely forgotten, Alfred Collins is examined for his contribution to the development of narrative through the adoption of the multi-scene chase format, while the highly regarded George Albert Smith of Hove is considered within social and geographical contexts, and examined in relation to the two pronounced comic themes of the grotesque body and gender issues as played through female servants.

American cross-currents are addressed by Ann-Marie Cook who discusses the transatlantic career of Florence Turner, the "Vitagraph Girl", best known for her face-pulling antics in *Daisy Doodad's Dial* (1914), and the ways in which Turner was re-created for the American market. The relationship between comedy and melodramatic theatrical performance is discussed by Trish Sheils in her essay on the film-of-the-play, *Trilby* (1914), in which the exaggerated theatrical performance of Sir Herbert Beerbohm Tree in particular mines a vein of humour inherent to George Du Maurier's text. Sheils discusses the extent to which melodramatic performance has been reinterpreted as a comedic style by recent audiences and critics, but argues against these texts being without humour in the first place. The American scholar Frank Scheide offers a valuable and detailed account of the career and work of Fred Karno at the interface between the music-hall and silent cinema. His research on the development and adaptation of specific sketches from stage to screen gives an insight into the relationship between performers and producers on both sides of the Atlantic, and the ways in which similar sketches were reinterpreted and refined over time for the new medium.

Michael Hammond offers a comprehensive study of the work of the popular, influential but relatively unknown British comedian Fred "Pimple" Evans, who made dozens of films during the 1910s, but has all but vanished into obscurity, a problem common to the majority of British silent stars. Betty Balfour and her character "Squibs", the subject of Judith McLaren's essay, have fared better than most in this respect, and McLaren's use of the contemporary trade press as a valuable research tool throws light onto how British stars were manufactured and promoted during this period.

Gerry Turvey examines the comic series as part of the vulgar popular entertainments of the period, taking as his focus the British and Colonial Kinematograph Company (B&C), a leading producer of the form. Christine Gledhill examines the collaborations between filmmaker Adrian Brunel and author A A Milne, in particular the sophisticated comedy produced by intertitles, understated performances and the knowing asides that these films frequently make to their audiences. Gledhill's research proves the need to revisit and reappraise 1920s British comedy features, many of which have lain untouched in the NFTVA for decades but are surprisingly modern in their humour.

Parody, as a pronounced tendency of British comic cinema, is the theme of Jamie Sexton's essay on filmmakers working on the fringes of mainstream cinema. Sexton also picks up the work of Brunel and Ivor Montagu whose films verge on the postmodern in terms of their "false authenticity", unabashed burlesquing of popular genres, playful eclecticism, and use of found and recycled footage. Sexton makes a convincing argument that 1920s British alternative film culture does not deserve its reputation for élitism, and instead serves as a fascinating challenge to the pomposity and rigidity of mainstream cinema. Both Gledhill and Sexton are aware of the financial restrictions on 1920s cinema, particularly compared with American films, and also of how British filmmakers succeeded in using their low budgets to ironic and comic advantage.

Cross-dressing, mistaken gender and sexual identities are key components of Amy Sargeant's work on the thematics of British screen comedy before the First World War, in which she identifies a significant number of incidents involving drag and cross-dressing. She traces the antecedents of this to the Victorian stage, but also offers further explanation in terms of misogyny (particularly at the expense of the suffragette movement), the comedy inherent in grotesque exaggeration, and subversion of the female physique. After useful excursions into Freud and Bergson and comparisons with latter-day cross-dressing comedians, Sargeant questions the extent to which this tendency resulted from the lack of female comic performers in British cinema during the 1910s.

In terms of star studies, Michael Williams' essay on Ivor Novello offers a revisionist insight into this complex performer and matinée idol, questioning the way in which critics have disparaged the star's work, and productively seeking a more substantive understanding of the "queer side" of his performance. Robert Murphy similarly redirects focus, asking new questions of the most well-known British films of the late silent period, and making for an awareness of the ignored comic qualities of Hitchcock's silent British cinema. And finally, Jenny Hammerton, archivist at Pathé, gives a brief description of the wealth of material in that particular collection, for which study is long overdue.

There are many conclusions to derive from this project and publication. The overall quality of comedy films from this period is uneven, and not all of the slapstick films elicit unbridled laughter; Britain produced no one to rival performers such as Arbuckle, Lloyd or Keaton. Many British film producers gave up the chase and simply avoided comedy altogether, but many of the surviving films surprise in the sophistication of their wit, their use of irony, and their modernity. There are fascinating glimpses of forgotten stars and lost films, and of the sheer volume of material begging to be examined and understood. This inaugural project is potentially the tip of a very big iceberg.

Thanks are due to the following: Broadway Cinema and staff, in particular Dave Pitt and the technical team; staff from the National Film and Television Archive and BFI Collections, including Bryony Dixon and Elaine Burrows; Luke McKernan from the British Universities Film and Video Council; and Christine Gledhill, Frank Gray, Mike Hammond, John Hawkridge, Paul Marygold, Frank Scheide and Trish Sheils for their help on the British Silent Cinema Weekend planning committee.

British Silent Comedy Films at the National Film and Television Archive

Bryony Dixon

When we consider the huge quantity of books, articles, theses, television documentaries and festivals dealing with silent American film comedy, it might seem surprising that so very little attention has been paid to British films from the same era. There are good reasons for this, not least of which is the iconic status of Charlie Chaplin (and, to some extent, the other top-grade American comics). When it is considered at all, British comedy has a lowly reputation, and generally has been dismissed as parochial and poorly produced, and very few people have ever seen any of the films. This is partly because the exhibition and study of silent cinema are more recent and less widespread than one would think, and also because the British material really does suffer in comparison with the American product. It is difficult enough to see prints of Buster Keaton or Harold Lloyd films, let alone the obscure remnants of a British industry that has left little trace in the popular imagination. But is it fair to compare the home-grown efforts of a nascent industry with the finely honed and prolific product of 1920s Hollywood? Is it reasonable to compare any comic at all with Chaplin, who was, by any standard, a phenomenon?

Faced with such negativity, it was with some trepidation that we decided on comedy as a theme for the second British Silent Cinema Weekend, but, as the weekend progressed, it became clear that our fears were groundless. Not only were the films interesting, but many of them were getting laughs. Of course, if you are serious about your Chaplins, Lupino Lanes or Stan Laurels, you would surely want to know something of the origins of their craft, and this is reason enough to consider the British comic films produced at a time when these artistes were working in the English music-hall. Several British performers went on from the music-hall to make comic films in both Britain and the United States, and there are a few examples of artistes performing their routines and sketches in front of the camera. The career of a comedian such as Lupino Lane can be traced from music-hall artiste through to film comedian in Britain, and finally film comedian of some note in Hollywood. So, whilst the British films may not compete with the American ones in terms of popularity, there are still good reasons to watch them, and they do offer their own rewards.

Another important reason for watching comic films is inherent in the nature of comedy itself. As a form, it enables us to peek behind the façade of social convention. The past is another country only until you can laugh with someone from 100 years ago. Laughter is about recognition, after all, and some things never change. Humour is a liberating device which allows full reign to the anarchism of the "naughty boys" of so many early comedies, and frees women from the constraints of 19th-century moral convention which informs most melodrama from

4

the period. Chrissie White in *Wife: The Weaker Vessel* (Hepworth, 1915) is a thoroughly modern girl no more limited in her capacity to have fun than anyone today. There is also plenty to study in British comedy itself. Watch some of the Brunel films of the 1920s and think of Monty Python's Flying Circus – the 1924 film *Crossing the Great Sagrada* could have been an episode of *Ripping Yarns*. Watch the "Pimple" skits and think of the comedy sketch shows on television today. Even the very earliest chase films might remind us of Benny Hill.

It is difficult to make scientific judgments about the comic films from this period as so few of them still exist. There are many reasons for the survival (or non-survival) of these films, most of which are well-known. Cinema has been seen as a disposable product during the course of its history, and Britain more than most countries has an innate snobbery about film in general and "low" comedy in particular; the British film industry was not sufficiently financially successful to overcome highbrow critical prejudice. But all artistic product has suffered from these attitudes, and archivists of all forms – books, fine art, music or the dramatic arts – struggle with their mission to preserve and record the artefacts. Film in particular suffers from aspects of its technical make-up; it can deteriorate quickly, and it is expensive and difficult to duplicate. Many of the surviving films in our collection are fragments or nth-generation duplicates losing much of their original quality in the process. Nitrate films were particularly vulnerable as the prints were often scrapped for their silver content. Films also take up a lot of space. After the commercial life of a film had ended, distributors wanted to get rid of them to make room for other product. The National Film and Television Archive (NFTVA) has relied upon donations from a variety of sources, principally film collectors and enthusiasts, but also laboratories, film studios, members of the public and sometimes the filmmakers themselves.

Sadly, the films discussed here are only a tiny proportion of the total made in the silent period, and we should ask the question: where are the missing appearances on film of the great music-hall performers Dan Leno, Marie Lloyd and George Robey? Where are the early films of Lupino Lane, Billy Merson and Charles Austin, which would help to flesh out our knowledge of their careers (and even possibly entertain). Where are the lost Fred Evans burlesques, such as *Pimple on Secret Service* or *Trilby by Pimple and Co* (1914), to go with our surviving fragment of *Trilby* (1914) with the great actor Sir Herbert Beerbohm Tree? Where, too, are the 1920s comedy drama features, of which so few survive, such as Walter Forde's *What Next?* (1928) or Betty Balfour in *Squibs Honeymoon* (1924)? We may well never know, but even now the films do turn up. A Walter Forde short, *Never Say Die* (1920), came to light only the other day...

The NFTVA has a collection of about 1500 British silent comedy titles. Most of these have been preserved and copied, and are accessible for screening or research viewing. We have deliberately kept the definition of comedy flexible. Briefly, the term covers straight comedy, slapstick, cartoons, comedy drama (i.e. dramas with some comic elements) and farce. The British Silent Comedy Catalogue (obtainable from the NFTVA), which we produced for the Weekend, was designed to create access to the NFTVA collections for anyone who wants to book to view or screen this rare and largely unknown material. It is intended as a practical guide and is still a work-in-progress. More work needs to be done by enthusiasts and students of the subject, as well as by the staff of the British Film Institute (BFI), but it is our hope that the "Weekend" will contribute to this body of research, and the aim is always to screen as much material as possible to enable those interested in the subject to see the films in context, projected onto a cinema screen, and presented with live music to an audience. With comedy in particular, this can radically change one's perception of the films. For example, when we screened the

"Pimple" films, people laughed. These had previously been considered poor because of the low production values and bizarre sense of humour, but they came across as genuinely funny with an audience, proof that we need to exhibit these films properly. That sense of the ridiculous does not come across half as well when sitting in the basement of the BFI watching them in silence on a viewing table.

Of course, there are British silent comedy films in other collections beyond the NFTVA, but the catalogue probably represents the largest collection of extant material, and, being a public body, the NFTVA has a commitment to making the films accessible for exhibitors and students of the subject. We hope that this book will help the films to become better-known and encourage further much-needed research.

How To Make *Ben Hur* Look Like an Epic

Luke McKernan

Comedy is cheap and, whilst drama's pretensions require the expense and effort of re-creating serious reality, poking fun comes as cheap as blowing a raspberry. A costly comedy film is too often one that has gone wrong somewhere. Charlie Chaplin famously said that all one needed to create comedy was "a park, a policeman and a pretty girl".[1] Monty Python's Flying Circus put paid to decades of portentous historical dramas when their Arthurian knights galloped by on pretend horses. And Pimple (Fred Evans), Britain's most popular comedian in the early years of cinema, made much the same point in his 1917 parody of the stage spectacular *The Whip*. The theatrical sensation of its age, *The Whip* boasted an on-stage rail crash and a climactic horse-race with real horses on a revolving stage. Pimple, a specialist in parody, with all of cinema's realism at his command, gives us the crash of a patently cardboard train, and stages the big race with jockeys riding one-man pantomime horses. Monty Python's only innovation was to dispense with any would-be horses at all.

The first distinctive feature of the British silent comedy film is its cheapness. Few spent lavishly on British silent films as a whole, and fewer still spent lavishly and well. For comedy, all that was needed was for a clown to perform some public misdemeanour and for a chase to ensue. The clown wreaks further havoc as he is pursued, until he is either cornered by his pursuers to exact their revenge, or (more commonly) he tricks them one more time and turns to the camera laughing. Such is the typical British comedy one-reeler of the pre-war period, where most British silent comedy films were concentrated, and the address to the audience is significant. The comedians were predominantly from the stage, with comic business and particular sketches well-honed from years of touring music-halls, and they naturally thrived on an audience reaction. They had to play to somebody, and the camera becomes the accomplice in the clown's misbehaviour, as he invites us to share in his joke and his victory.

The themes of the chase, the socially disruptive clown, the debt to the music-hall stage, and the playing to the camera are all present to some degree or other in European and American comedies of the same period. Among the peculiarly British qualities to be noted are a fascination with authority and class (inevitably), a lack of sentiment, and a delight in the absurd. The heroes of so many early British comedies are young boys or tramps, and the victims are so often policemen, teachers, the pompous and those in authority. The archetypal British one-reel comedy is James Williamson's *Our New Errand Boy* (1907), in which the boy creates havoc when he is asked to sweep out a shop, setting various adult figures against one another, before they realise that he is the culprit and give chase. In doing so they only become more dishevelled, more ridiculous, and in the end he traps them all in a chicken coop, and the film ends with a close-up of the boy laughing broadly. The sympathies of the audience, frequently comprised of juveniles and predominantly working-class, and subject normally to being placed firmly at the bottom of a rigidly stratified society at this time, are firmly with the boy who ridicules his betters and gets away with it. The rules of polite society and social aspiration are similarly flouted by the fearsome "Daddy's Little Did'ums" in Clarendon's series of that title, and by the two young girls in Cecil Hepworth's anarchic "Tilly the Tomboy" series.

British comedy is also a comedy without pathos. It will always be a matter of speculation how Chaplin might or might not have flourished in film if he had remained in Britain, but it seems fairly certain that there would have been little encouragement of his more lachrymose tendencies. The gags are broad, unsubtle, ridiculous and cruel, and generally lacking in any grace. To pursue the Chaplin connection a little further, look at Sam T Poluski, a comedian trained, as Chaplin was, by music-hall producer Fred Karno, in *Nobby the New Waiter* (1913). See how the comedy of a man on roller skates might come from the same Karno stable, but that in *The Rink* (1916) Chaplin gives us a comedy of infinitely greater subtlety, character and humour. For many British comedies are not all that funny. They are frequently merely coarse sight gags, with the clown laughing more at his own mischief than the audience may feel inclined to do. It is hard to believe that any audience ever found the Bamforth Company's Winky (Reggie Switz), for instance, as funny as he believed himself to be.

Yet, there were comedies of greater subtlety, and many of them were provided by the inventive Clarendon Film Company. If we only knew the names of the players in the films of this elusive but inventive company of the pre-war era, we might gain a greater purchase on their accomplished and socially aware comedies, which deftly pile absurdity upon absurdity. Excellent examples include the gleeful reversal of the sexes in the suffragette satire *Milling the Militants* (1913), the inventive calamities of *A Glass of Goat's Milk* (1909), and the naughty cross-dressing of *Love and the Varsity* (1913). Men dressed as women is another distinctive trait of British silent comedy, inherited as usual from the music-hall stage (and Chaplin performed *en travesti* in three of his American comedies). This is seen most simply in the chase comedies, where the female roles are often played by men, which may have been as much a matter of decorum as a source of humour (for example, Clarendon's *Three Maiden Ladies and a Bull* [1913]). But a stronger theme is the man dressed as a woman who is thereby able to act wildly with impunity, breaking down the rules for just a short while, as so many of these comedies do. Notable examples are Cricks and Martin's *Lord Algy's Beauty Show* (1908) and Gaumont's lubricious *How Percy Won the Beauty Competition* (1909).

British silent comedies therefore offer little acts of rebellion or social disruption on behalf of the circumscribed or less fortunate. What British films generally failed to do was to develop beyond this into the 1920s. The comparative lack of British comedies, good or bad, in the 1920s is notable. There are some individual features of note, such as the engaging Leslie Henson farce, *Tons of Money* (1924), or the energetic Monty Banks in *Adam's Apple* and *Weekend Wives* (both 1928), but in general there appears to have been a reluctance to engage in serious comedy production, partly because American product satisfied audience needs and desires, and partly because of a likely snobbery among certain British producers who felt that mere comedy was beneath their dignity. Indeed, a false idea of dignity hampered British film production for many years.

Three names from this period stand out, however. Walter Forde made two-reeler knockabout comedies in the American vein, and showed invention and the ability to sustain his ideas over the length of a feature film, notably in *Would You*

Believe It? (1929). He had his following, as Pimple had had in the previous decade, but lacked a strong comic character and would eventually discover his true talent behind the camera in the 1930s. Adrian Brunel made comedies of a very different order, although they are not so far away from Pimple in their delight in parody and in pinpointing the ridiculous. But Brunel had nothing to do with the music-hall tradition, and made dilettante comedies such as *The Bump* and *Bookworms* (both 1920), where the heroes and heroines achieve their small conquests among polite society, quietly conquering its absurdities in the manner of a P G Wodehouse story. Brunel developed his comedy in parodies of newsreels, travelogues and other genres in short films that delighted select London audiences, but he always remained a restricted talent with a narrow frame of reference. Lastly, there was Betty Balfour, an actress who gave comic performances, rather than a comedienne as such, but her bubbly, optimistic character, especially in the four *Squibs* films of cockney comedy, made her very popular. Distinctively British in style, she successfully mined a vein of sentiment that largely eluded other British comedy performers.

Overall, the British silent comedy struggled to find a style and an audience that would help it to compete with more polished efforts from Europe and especially America. Chaplin and Stan Laurel came from the same Karno stable as so many British comedians of this period, but it was in America that their talents flourished and they became universally popular. British comedies all too seldom found that popular touch – only Pimple, Walter Forde and Betty Balfour became strong favourites as comedy performers among British cinema audiences. Instead, mostly anonymous and interchangeable comedians indulge in small bouts of anarchy and assaults on convention. The best of British silent comedy delights in misrule, in bringing the grand down to earth, from scandalous boys who ridicule their schoolmasters, to Pimple as Napoléon leading his troops to Waterloo station, to Adrian Brunel crossing the Great Sagrada desert in his back garden. *Monty Python and the Holy Grail* was advertised with the immortal line, "Makes *Ben Hur* look like an epic". There were silent *Ben Hurs* as well, and British silent comedies gleefully worked to much the same motto. Comedy may be cheap, but it gives you value for your money.

Note

[1]   Charles Chaplin, *My Autobiography* (Harmondsworth: Penguin Books, 1966): 159.

British Comedy Films in the Silent Period: A Production Survey

Tony Fletcher

1898-1912

In 1898, comedy became a crucial genre for film production in Britain. Robert Paul, Birt Acres, G A Smith and James Williamson had all produced comedies between 1896 and 1898 – with Paul being the most active, making thirteen comedy films in 1897-98, including *Our New General Servant* (1898), which innovatively used subtitles in four of its scenes. Cecil Hepworth joined the pioneers in 1899, and his various companies would be responsible for more comedies than any other company during the silent period. At the end of the decade, however, the Warwick Trading Company was the leading producer of comedy films, using popular performers such as Will Evans, Harry Tate and Fred Poplar. Few of the comic films of the 19th century survive.

Hepworth released ten comedy films in 1900, some famously with trick effects, such as *The Explosion of a Motor Car* and *How It Feels To Be Run Over*. Paul's *The Countryman and the Cinematograph* and Williamson's *The Big Swallow* (both 1901) again demonstrated the skills of British filmmakers and the importance of comedy in the development of film technique. Warwick maintained production with films for the popular music-hall performers Dan Leno and Arthur Conquest, and were joined in 1902 by the important Gaumont Company which, within a year, became the leading producer of comedy films, releasing 24 in 1903, none of which has so far been traced. Other significant producers of the period include Hepworth (*The Unclean World*), Williamson (*The Dear Boys Home for the Holidays*), G A Smith (*Mary Jane's Mishap*), Mitchell and Kenyon (*Diving Lucy*), Urban (*Cheese Mites*) (all 1903) and William Haggar, who commenced production with comedienne Mog and her character "Mary". In 1905, the high point of production in Britain for the early period, 164 comedies were released by fourteen companies: Gaumont contributed 48 and Hepworth 25. Only four of the latter's films survive, including *Prehistoric Peeps* and *What the Curate Really Did*, while, disappointingly, none of the comedies from Clarendon, Paul or Urban for that year has been traced, including the historic record of a Fred Karno sketch, *A Raid on a Club*, completed by Walturdaw.

Comedies remained a staple of film production for the remainder of the decade, although a minority of the films survive for assessment. A new high for comedy production was reached in 1910 when 168 films were released. A marked feature of comic production in the new decade was the series: Hepworth, the dominant producer of comedies that year with 54, commenced its *Tilly* series; Clarendon had its popular *Daddy's Did'ums* series; Cricks and Martin (C and M) presented Fred Evans as "A Dandy" and Charlie Bolton as "Scroggins"; and B&C

started its *Snorky* series with Bill Haley, while Nelson Keys appeared as "Drowsy Dick". The production of comedies continued to expand in the 1910s, with 194 films released by thirteen companies in 1911, and 242 films produced by 27 companies in 1912; only sixteen of all these films are known to be extant. Hepworth retained a consistently high level of comedy production, and introduced its *Hawkeye* series with Hay Plumb and two series featuring Harry Buss as "Lieutenant Lilly" and "Poorluck". Director Lewin Fitzhamon left Hepworth to set up his own company, Fitz, making comedy films with the two Royston children, and Constance Somers as her character "Flapper". Britain's leading comic star of the 1910s, Fred Evans, and his enormously popular character "Pimple", first appeared this year in films put out by Ecko, although he soon moved to feature for Folly.

American producers were also active in comedy film production in Britain by this time, with Vitagraph contributing two films with John Bunny. Edison also made some films in England in 1912, of which *A Suffragette In Spite of Himself* survives.

1913-19

This period was dominated by Fred Evans who made an astonishing 99 comic films for Folly in only two years, 1913 and 1914, of which eight have survived. Pre-eminent were the series featuring "Pimple" and "Raffles", made with his brother Joe, and a speciality was pastiches of popular stories such as *Broncho Pimple, The House of Distemperly, The Battle of Gettysownback* (all 1914) and *A Study in Skarlit* (1915), with his uncle Will Evans as Professor Moratorium, and Fred as Sherlockz Holmz. Next to "Pimple", "Winky" was the most popular comic character in this period, played by the largely forgotten Reggie Switz. In 1914, he appeared in 47 films produced by the Bamforth Company, Yorkshire and directed by Cecil Birch who, unusually, received credit in some of the titles.

The firm of Cricks and Martin was a major producer of comic films in this period, and continued to be so after the two partners split up and formed their own separate companies. Both George Howard Cricks and John Howard Martin had worked for Paul in the early years of the century. Together and separately, C and M produced 130 comedies in 1913-14, of which fourteen are extant. These included several series: *Mike Murphy* (1914/15), *Boots* (1915) with Edouard Musto, and *Little Willie* (1913) with Roy Royston.

In his unpublished autobiography, David Aylott describes how four films a week were made at C and M.[1] Plot outlines were provided by Aylott and A E Coleby, approved by Cricks and Martin, and the films were shot around Mitcham, south London. The principal actors were paid seven shillings and sixpence and other performers five shillings, with one shilling and sixpence for travelling expenses to Mitcham. All were treated to bread and cheese for lunch, and beer, mineral water or tea. Production was rapid and the completed films were sold two days after shooting: Monday and Wednesday were put aside for shooting, and Wednesday and Friday for selling.

Throughout the 1910s, numerous music-hall performers had their acts recorded on film. These included Harry Lauder, George Robey, Will Evans, Nelson Keys, Mark Melford, George Formby Snr, George Mozart, Marie Lloyd and Fred Kitchen. A G P Huntley film, *Basil the Brainless* (1915), survives. There was also a predictable spate of Chaplin impersonations and pastiches, and Leslie Hatton impersonated him in three films: *Chaplie Charlin's Special Constable, Young Charlie's Half Day* and *Crazed as Charlie* (all 1915). Florence Turner, Walter Forde and Leslie Henson all took off the great Hollywood star, although none of these films is known to have survived.

The First World War had a great impact on British film production, as resources were put to the war effort. Many of the companies producing comics in the early 1910s has ceased production by 1916. Although Fred Evans joined up for a period, he was eventually declared unfit for active service and continued making "Pimple" films for various companies: 27 for Phoenix, and 37 for Piccadilly, a company run by two Americans, Charles Weston and Arthur Finn, with a studio in Bayswater, London. The pair also put out the following series: *Lemon and Dash*, *The Terrible Twins* (both 1914/15), and *Mr and Mrs Piecan* (1915) with Joe and Geraldine Evans. Only six of the Piccadilly films have been traced.

Other firms that struggled on with comedy filmmaking included Bamforth (68 in 1915) with its series of "Lily", "Alf" and "Scotty" comedies; Cricks, which released a series of spoof Shakespeare films featuring Will Kellino; Martin with its staple of trick and comic shorts; Clarendon with its series of "Jack Spratt", "Maudie" and "Daddy's Did'ums" comedies, but which was soon taken over by the renter HARMA; and Hepworth, still making arguably the best comedies, although on a reduced scale. The Walton-on-Thames producer released 113 comedies in 1913-14, but only 38 comedies during 1915-16, of which thirteen survive. His leading comic in this period was Tom Butt who made a series of ten "Tubby" films with Violet Hopson – several having a propaganda theme. Some of the leading comic performers also involved themselves in production. The much-travelled and experienced Will Kellino joined with Billy Merson to form a company called Homeland: Merson lost money attempting to rival Chaplin in burlesques such as *The Terrible Tec* (1916), imitating Sherlock Holmes; while Kellino enjoyed success in a series featuring Lupino Lane as "Nipper", two of which survive. Kellino made a total of 51 comedies for his Ecko Company, of which only one is extant. Kellino was a significant figure in British screen comedy, a popular performer, prolific producer and successful director who graduated to feature-length comedies in the 1920s, and continued in sound films in the early 1930s. In addition, American star Florence Turner, the "Vitagraph Girl", set up the Turner Films Company in Britain, and enjoyed considerable success in the 1910s with films such as *Daisy Doodad's Dial* (1914).

Many other companies made some comedies in the 1910s, but few of these films have survived to allow assessment. Special mention should be made of four women filmmakers who were active in this period: Ivy Close with her own studio at Esher; Ethyle Batley working for B&C; Alice Rosenthal with her own A R Company; and Nell Emerald, a producer at Brightonia. The latter is best remembered now as the aunt of star Ida Lupino.

1920-29

The 1910s had seen a decisive shift from the cruder form of the street comic to a more sophisticated "studio comedy", and after the war this, in turn, fed into a greater emphasis on feature-length comedies. So, for example, in 1920, 95 comedy films included thirteen features, while over a third of comic films in 1921 were features, an impressive total of 22 films. The survival rate of the 1920s comedies is disappointing at around 20%, although the figure for feature comedies is a more reassuring 35%. As the decade progressed, film production in Britain assumed ever more desperate straits, and this was inevitably reflected in the preparation and release of comic titles. The production of comedy features fell persistently between 1922 and 1926 to a dismal two titles; numbers picked up again, falteringly, after the issuing of protective legislation in 1927, and production recovered to sixteen comedy features and 38 comic shorts in 1928. And this, the last complete year of silent film production in Britain, represents the best year for survival of titles in the decade, with 35% of all comedy films having been located.

Among the most successful comedy features of the period were the *Squibs* films directed by George Pearson and starring Betty Balfour. Another emergent director was Walter Forde, who had made three comic shorts for Castle Films in 1920, appeared as a comic performer in 1921 in two films for director Joe Bamberger, but was again directing himself a year later in four comedies that survive. He remained an important producer and director of comedy in the 1920s with his "Super Comedies" productions, and a comparatively good proportion of his films survive. The new maturity of British screen comedy was apparent in the literate and witty parodies of Adrian Brunel – films far more advanced in their comedic structures and sophisticated handling than the crude burlesques of Fred Evans which continued to appear in the 1920s. Remarkably, all four of Brunel's shorts produced by his Minerva Company in 1920, featuring Leslie Howard and C Aubrey Smith, survive. In 1923, Brunel sent up George Robey's *Chu-Chin-Chow* as *Two Chinned-Chow*, and later in the decade he parodied various film forms: the travel film in *Crossing the Great Sagrada* (1924), and the newsreel in *Pathetic Gazette* (1924) and *A Typical Budget* (1925).

The first sound comedy shorts were produced on De Forest's Phonofilm in 1926, and featured Billy Merson, Nervo and Knox, Dick Henderson and Gwen Farrar. A De Forest short, *His Rest Day*, starring Matthew Boulton, is the only comedy film to survive from 1927. A better record is attained by the 1928 productions on Phonofilm, with productions for Billy Bennett, Moore Marriott, George Robey and Robb Wilton. Ten comedy shorts were also produced by British Sound Film Productions directed by Hugh Croise with Wilkie Bard, Horace Kenney and John Henry; the company managed fifteen shorts in 1929, of which two survive.[2]

Amidst the mounting difficulties in film production, several companies and individuals stand out for their contribution to screen comedy. Gaumont, Ideal, Samuelson, Nettlefold and Stoll were significant production centres, while popular performers included Harry Hearty (the English Fatty Arbuckle), another "Fatty", Kimber Phillips, Queenie Thomas, Nelson Keys, Johnny Butt and George Robey. Prominent comic filmmakers included Will Kellino, Sinclair Hill, Widgey Newman, Gaston Quiribet and Maurice Elvey. Finally, mention should be made of the filming of three Karno sketches in 1923 by Lucien Egrot and Albert Brouett: *Early Birds*, *Jail Birds* and the seminal *Mumming Birds*. After all, the comic routines and methods of Karno had been so influential on the practice of screen comedy through such admirers as Charlie Chaplin, and remain a crucial British legacy to silent film comedy in general.

Notes

This survey is indebted to Denis Gifford's invaluable *The British Film Catalogue 1895-1985: A Reference Guide* (Newton Abbot; London: David & Charles, 1986).

[1]   David Aylott's unpublished memoirs are held at the National Film and Television Archive (NFTVA), London.

[2]   Recently, a cache of De Forest Phonofilms has come to light which greatly increases the number extant.

Alfred Collins:
Britain's Forgotten Filmmaker

Barry Anthony

1903 represented a high-watermark for the British influence on American and European films. A number of directors began to utilise the dramatic and comic potential of multi-scene chases, a device that was so important to the development of narrative films. There had been earlier limited chases such as those depicted in the Lumières' *L'Arroseur arrosé* (*Watering the Gardener*, 1895), Edison's *Fake Beggar* (1898) and James Williamson's three-shot *Stop Thief* (1901), but Frank Mottershaw's eight-scene *A Daring Daylight Burglary* (April 1903) was clearly a new departure. During the same year, Mottershaw produced several chases whose violence and rapidly unfolding action were rivalled by William Haggar's *A Desperate Poaching Affray* (July 1903). The introduction of such sensational productions in the United States soon led to the first American chase movies: Biograph's *The Escaped Lunatic* and Edison's *The Great Train Robbery* (both November 1903). The influence of Mottershaw and Haggar on the development of the fiction film is now widely recognised, but that of a third director, Alfred Collins, is largely overlooked. During 1903 and 1904, several Gaumont chase films made in Britain were widely circulated in Europe and the United States. In his use of frantic and prolonged action, subjective camerawork, close-ups and panning shots, Alfred Collins did as much as any other director to lay the foundations for a comic chase tradition.

Collins, director of over 200 films for Gaumont in the 1902-10 period, was remembered by the company's Managing Director, A C Bromhead:

> Our first producer was Alfred Collins, not Collins of Drury Lane, but a member of Kate Carney's staff, who took quite a number of successful short films for us. Some of them were really elaborate, such as 'The Curfew Shall Not Ring To-night,' 'Napoleon and the Sailor'; but Collins's mind, in his earlier efforts, leaned much to chases, and he gave us many exciting ones, such as 'The Pickpocket,' 'A Runaway Match,' 'Welshed at the Derby,' and 'A Leg of Mutton Chases'...I have only mentioned a very few, but Collins turned out dozens of films for us.[1]

Filming at Gaumont's open-air studio at Champion Hill, Dulwich, in the streets of south-east London, and on occasional visits to South Coast resorts, Alf was assisted by his wife Maud Lucy Collins, who not only appeared alongside him in many productions, but also acted as script supervisor and prompter. Alf's background provided considerable experience of the world of Victorian popular entertainment. His younger brother Charles William Collins (1875-1923) was one of the music-hall's most prolific songwriters, providing such classics as Marie Lloyd's "Don't Dilly

Dally on the Way", Lily Morris' "Why Am I Always the Bridesmaid?" and Harry Champion's "Boiled Beef and Carrots". Another brother, George Collins, was a well-known songwriter and female impersonator, while a sister, Nellie Cotter, was also a variety performer billed as "The One With a Voice".

Alf was born in 1865 or 1866, and made his stage debut, probably at the Surrey Theatre, south London, at the age of eighteen. Another early appearance was at the Lyceum in 1884, when Mary Anderson and William Terriss starred in a famous version of *Romeo and Juliet*. During the 1880s and 1890s, he played minor roles in productions starring some of the greatest names of Victorian theatre, including Henry Irving, George Alexander, Cyril Maude, Fred Terry and Julia Neilson. In 1902, he appeared with his idol, the leading music-hall comedian Dan Leno, in the Drury Lane Theatre pantomime *Mother Goose*. Alf played one of three comic policemen in the harlequinade sequence, a seemingly significant role considering the number of ill-treated policemen depicted in his films. If we are seeking theatrical antecedents for the film chase, we need look no further than the Victorian harlequinade, a riotous postscript to the main pantomime in which constantly frustrated policemen pursued clown and pantaloon through a series of rapidly changing scenes.

Sometime before 1902, Alf had worked for R W Paul and for the British Mutoscope and Biograph Company. After joining Gaumont, Alf combined filmmaking with live stage appearances with Kate Carney's music-hall troupe of coster comedians. Costers – London street vendors – often featured in Alf's films, although, unlike policemen, these rough-and-ready, fiercely independent traders were portrayed with considerable sympathy. In fact, his films often depicted socially deprived groups hitting back at the forces of authority. In *The Eviction* (1904), the police are soaked with water, while the bailiff is pushed away in a wheelbarrow by a group of Irish tenants. An advertisement for one of Alf's most important chase films, *The Pickpocket, or A Chase Through London* (October 1903), promised "Robbery, Struggles, Fights, Chases, Escapes, and Policemen's Blood Galore".[2] In *The Coster's Wedding* (1904), Gaumont stressed that the cast and location were totally authentic: "absolutely a real coster picture, taken in costermongerland with real costers".[3] Alf's keenness to film in actual locations led, in 1904, to him, his cameraman Arthur James Porter and A C Bromhead being prosecuted for obstruction. Collins and Bromhead were each fined ten shillings, with the magistrate's admonition of "the next thing we shall have shall be a motor accident in Piccadilly for the purpose of being taken on the cinematograph, and brought out at the Empire the same evening".[4] In many ways, Alf's anti-Establishment viewpoint serves as a refreshing alternative to the suburban *Angst* of Cecil Hepworth, a cheerfully amoral antidote to the anxious frock-coated gentlemen guarding their children against theft by gypsies, and protecting their property against tramps, burglars and random explosions.

Alf's output was extensive, but relatively few of his films are known to have survived. Of the missing titles, perhaps the most important is *Welshed, a Derby Day Incident* (June 1903). From Gaumont catalogue descriptions we know that the film started with a panning shot of the Epsom racecourse, and contained not only an extended chase sequence, but also a subjective view with a bookmaker watching the horse-race through binoculars. From 1909, it would be interesting to locate *The Martyrdom of Adolph Beck*, an intriguing piece of faction which, at 1630', was the longest British film produced to that time. It is quite likely that Collins also directed Gaumont's 1240' version of *Romeo and Juliet* (1908) starring the well-known actor Godfrey Tearle.

Sufficient films survive, however, to demonstrate that Collins was an innovative director whose influence on international filmmaking has not been widely recognised. Although he worked mainly with the cameraman Arthur Porter, it seems likely that he also made films with Herbert Blaché, an important figure in the French and American film worlds, and husband of one of the first female film directors, Alice Guy. Charles Musser has written that, from 1903, British story films such as Haggar's *A Desperate Poaching Affray*, R W Paul's *Trailed by Bloodhounds*, Mottershaw's *A Daring Daylight Burglary* and Collins' *The Runaway Match* "conveyed a sensationalistic energy that American and French producers soon emulated".[5] We know from copyright records that Collins' films were also issued in the United States by the American Biograph Company from 1903.

Several of Collins' most important films are preserved in the Library of Congress Paper Print Collection, but copies have unfortunately not been obtained for the National Film and Television Archive (NFTVA). *The Runaway Match; or, Married by Motor* refines the chase structure to show the same incident as perceived by the pursued and the pursuers. The film also includes a remarkable close-up of a wedding ring being placed on a woman's hand. Collins appears to have developed the close-up for dramatic effect, employing an emblematic pistol firing at the beginning of *Raid on a Coiner's Den* (1904), and a shot of a High Court warrant in *The Eviction*. *The Pickpocket* (copyrighted in the United States in December 1903) presents a complex twelve-shot chase, in which a swelling crowd hunt a young criminal along roads, through houses and over fences. The final struggle ends after a constable has been hurled from the top of a towering woodpile. Of the thirteen identified films by Collins in the NFTVA, *The Tale of a Coat* (1905), *The Missing Legacy; or, The Story of a Brown Hat* (1906) and *Oh, That Cat* (1907) depend on extended chases for their humour. Alf's usual attitude towards the police is displayed in *Night Duty* (1904), with a flirtatious constable being put painfully in his place by a woman with a hot poker. In *When Extremes Meet* (1905), Alf and Maud portray a pair of tipsy costers whose boisterous behaviour upsets a middle-class couple and leads to the arrest of a clergyman who attempts to bring the warring parties together.

Following his abandonment of filmmaking shortly before the First World War, Alf continued to appear with Kate Carney, also returning to legitimate drama with Sir John Martin Harvey's company in the 1920s. By the time of his death in 1952, his contribution to the development of the fiction film had been almost entirely forgotten, and a subsequent generation of film historians have equally failed to acknowledge Collins' importance as a pioneer of British film comedy.

Notes

[1]   A C Bromhead, "Reminiscences of the British Film Trade", *Proceedings of the British Kinematograph Society* 21 (1933): 13.

[2]   *The Era* 67: 3406 (2 January 1904): 41.

[3]   L Gaumont and Co, *Elge Original Film Subjects* June 1904: 71.

[4]   *The British Journal of Photography* 29 April 1904: 359-360.

[5]   Charles Musser, *The Emergence of Cinema: The American Screen to 1907* (New York: Charles Scribner's Sons, 1990): 365.

George Albert Smith's Comedies of 1897

Frank Gray

From 1897 to 1903, George Albert Smith produced a number of remarkable film comedies, largely within the grounds of his pleasure garden in Hove. These films have very clear correspondences with contemporary humour as found in popular graphics, the music-hall stage, pantomime and other films, and they demonstrate his awareness of both comic timing and the temporal aspects of film. This essay is a study of two surviving comedies from 1897, Smith's first full year of film production and only a year since the beginnings of the new medium's commercial life in 1896. In 1897, he completed 32 films for retail sale. They were a mixture of non-fiction and fiction subjects, each one a single shot of about a minute in length. Together, they provided a potential exhibitor with a very balanced and intriguing programme of animated photographs. Of these, 23 were non-fiction, consisting of actualities (everyday scenes) and topicalities (specific events) shot across Sussex and London, with subjects such as a train arriving at Hove Station, amusing scenes at the Southwick Regatta, the Brighton Sea-Going Electric Car, his two-film record of the Queen's Diamond Jubilee, and a three-film portrait of Ellen Terry.

Of the nine works of fiction, titles and catalogue descriptions indicate that eight of these were comedies. They are, in chronological order: *Hanging Out the Clothes* – "Master, Mistress, and Maid. Very comic"; *The Lady Barber, or Comic Shaving* – "What we shall come to, and how to make the best of a 'bad job'"; *The Miller and the Sweep* – "A dusty fight between soot and flour; windmill at work in background"; *Comic Face* – "Old man drinking glass of beer, old women taking snuff"; *Weary Willie* – "Tramp engaged to beat carpets, beats employer by mistake – rewarded by pail of water"; *The X Rays* – "The Professor turns his apparatus upon the lovers and makes a startling revelation"; *Making Sausages* – "Live cats and dogs put into a machine, sausages come out. Four cooks. Always goes well"; and *Tipsy, Topsy, Turvey* – "The reveller's return from his club". Of these films, only *Hanging Out the Clothes*, *The Miller and the Sweep* and the first part of *Comic Face* have survived.[1]

These comic narratives present various transgressions of class, gender, morality and, more generally, the world of late-Victorian bourgeois society. We encounter illicit kissing, gender reversal, physical fighting, grotesque behaviour, the act of disrespecting one's employer, parodies of new technology and food production, and excessive consumption of alcohol. In a Freudian sense, they represent the relaxation of conscious control in favour of the unconscious. They become moments of liberty, operating almost in a coercive manner by countering dominant standards of behaviour. As comic narratives, the comic effects are the products of these transgressions and, invariably, the punishment which sometimes follows as a result. Like all comedy and all narratives, they are the products of history. These films were produced and consumed with an understanding of other narratives and an awareness of relevant fields of knowledge.

This comic work was also determined by the nature of the new medium. The films were created within very real and interrelated temporal and technological constraints. They could be no more than a minute in length, a duration set by the maximum length of unexposed film which could be held in the camera. Except for *The X Rays*, which employed stop-motion, all these films needed to be designed as a single continuous shot.[2] The comic event had to be prepared and delivered within these parameters. These films by Smith serve as a necessary and significant prelude to his development of the multi-shot edited film from 1899.

Hanging Out the Clothes

All of Smith's 1897 film comedies were shot out of doors, and, together with costumes and props, they worked within a realist aesthetic to gave contemporary viewers a clear and familiar correspondence between the filmed scene and the everyday world. *Hanging Out the Clothes* was made at St Ann's Well and Wild Garden in Hove on 20 September 1897.[3] Smith acquired the lease to this property in 1892. For about a decade, St Ann's provided Smith with a relatively large inner-town property on the border between Brighton and Hove which lent itself to the many activities required to make a successful pleasure garden. He organised afternoon teas and children's sports, built a monkey house, and employed a "gypsy fortune-teller". It was also the perfect site for filmmaking, film processing and film exhibition. In 1897, the Pump Room was converted into a space for film developing and printing. The grounds of St Ann's, from that same year, provided him with an ideal location for filmmaking. The usual site for this work was a clearing which faced due south, an area which was the highest part of the garden. This was the location used for *Hanging Out the Clothes*.

Smith's fiction films in the years 1897-1903 were largely comedies and adaptations of popular fairy tales and stories. His work within these genres was influenced by his wife Laura Bayley. Her life in the popular theatre before 1897, particularly in pantomime and comic revues, placed Smith in intimate contact with an experienced actress who understood visual comedy and the interests of typical seaside audiences. This complemented his background in mesmerism and the magic lantern. With Blanche, Florence and Eva, she was one of the four Bayley sisters. Together, they had worked for many years in the theatre company operated by, and named after, J D Hunter, featuring in his annual productions at the Brighton Aquarium. In September 1894, for example, the Bayleys were the stars of Hunter's *Babes in the Wood*. The *Brighton Herald* commented: "The Robin Hood of Miss Laura Bayley is a distinctly comely and cheery Robin Hood".[4] Laura appeared in the majority of Smith's fiction films, becoming one of the most important actresses in early British cinema.

In *Hanging Out the Clothes*, Laura was cast as the maid. Her fellow players in this film were Mr and Mrs Tom Green. The relevant entry in Smith's cash book notes that they were paid ten shillings for their services as the master and mistress.[5] Smith would regularly use Tom Green as the male lead in his films, usually opposite Laura. Also like Laura, Tom Green was a familiar Brighton comic actor. His local profile was particularly high in early 1897. As well as performing as the clown in the Aquarium's pantomime *Cinderella* (January 1897), he directed and performed in his own play *Jack O' Clubs* at the Gaiety Theatre in February. The *Sussex Daily News* relished his work in this production:

There was a large audience at the Brighton Gaiety Theatre last night for the first of a week's performances of Mr Tom Green's sensational play, *Jack O' Clubs*. The play is remarkably well written, the characters are well drawn, the dialogue is crisp and amusing...Mr Tom Green has an interesting part, or rather series of parts, as Horatio Plantagenet Peppermint, a mystery, Dick Devereux the convict, Mrs Jemima Jones, Wang See, the Heathen Chinee [sic], and Jimmy Johnson, the old jockey. This means, of course, a number of disguises, which are assumed and thrown off with wonderful rapidity. One of the best of these is that of Mrs. Jemima Jones, a good old lady who sings a little song about the way people enjoyed themselves when George the Third was King. The Chinaman is also a good disguise, and the effect of all these changes is heightened by the fact that they are not introduced merely to display the cleverness of the actor, but really have an important bearing on the plot.[6]

With Bayley and Green, Smith had experienced and accomplished performers who supported him in the creation of these film comedies.

A 1900 catalogue description conveys the action of *Hanging Out the Clothes* very succinctly and, if we assume that these are Smith's own words, captures his understanding of this comedy: "The busy maiden hanging out the clothes is tickled by the master, who entices her behind a sheet. 'Missus' returns from shopping, looks for maid, sees the pair of feet beneath the hanging sheet, tears it down – tableau. Maid flies, master 'faces the music' and doubtless makes rapid progress towards baldness in consequence".[7]

Two versions of this film exist at the National Film and Television Archive (NFTVA). The first version is very much a rehearsal. Green, as the master, acts in a hyperactive manner, with frequent arm and leg gestures drawn from the tradition of stage melodrama. Obviously, they are intended to connote his sexual excitement, especially his little kicks. The creation of the final tableau is poorly organised. The maid, played by Laura, is uncertain where to stand, and ends up in shadow. These comments can be made because these are the very issues which are addressed in the second version. Here Smith sharpens the action so that it is crisper and therefore more effective. Green's movements become much more restrained and Smith shortens the concluding action of the hair-pulling. And, as part of this final tableau, Laura confidently takes up a position in the background which is in the light, and balanced against the action of the master and the mistress in the foreground. The existence of these two versions enables us to have some grasp of the preparations required for the production of the final film. Smith, Bayley and Green worked to ensure that the comic action was carefully tailored to the real constraints of a single shot, one-minute film comedy. They were producing their concept of film comedy, as opposed to stage comedy.

As a comic narrative, *Hanging Out the Clothes* is a very conventional depiction of male transgression within marriage. In the exposition stage, the master of the household takes advantage of his wife's absence and seduces a member of his staff. However, his actions as a libertine can only occur for a few seconds as he is interrupted by his wife's return and her discovery of his infidelity. His desire for illicit sexual pleasure results in pain. This is a narrative climax which signifies his moral weakness and his wife's assertion of correctness. The comedy is the product of witnessing both his desire and his punishment, with his wife functioning as a domestic legislator of acceptable behaviour. Both these stages in the drama are represented by physical actions which are delivered for comic effect. To maintain a sense of moral order in this fictional world, *his* desire needs to be actively contained and controlled by *her* vigilance. John Barnes has found a possible contemporary source for the film. In a photograph published in *Photograms of the Year 1896* and entitled "What the Missus Saw", a wife recoils in horror as she sees, in silhouette, her husband kiss a woman behind a sheet on the clothes line.[8]

The Miller and the Sweep

This single shot, one-minute comedy was produced on location in front of Brighton's Race Hill Mill. In a carefully and beautifully framed master-shot in which the sails of the mill turn in the background, the film commences with the miller walking directly towards the camera. Both he and the mill are centrally positioned within the frame. His progress towards the front of this scene is clearly delineated by the fact that the dark surface of the mill's tower provides a graphic contrast with his white apparel. His journey forward, towards our point of view, is halted by his collision with the sweep who has entered from the left. Their physical contact instantly precipitates their physical fight. They wrestle each other to the ground and then literally fall out of the frame. They are followed by the "villagers", a crowd of adults and children, who enter from the right-hand side and run across the bottom of the frame, following the direction taken by the miller and the sweep. The film concludes without a resolution, like the images on a magic lantern panoramic slipping slide.

As an early example of visual comedy designed for the film camera, *The Miller and the Sweep* creates its comic effect through a combination of staging and timing. Not only is the action staged so that visually it dominates the centre of the film frame, but also the cathartic violence breaks out within seconds of the start of the film. The literal eruption of the action creates an unexpected visual shock. Smith's creation of this surprise was the film's single comic device.

The film's production was carefully planned. Entries in Smith's cash book reveal that he made two versions of the film. The first was shot on 24 July 1897.[9] The absence of any evidence of sales of the resulting print and the need to restage the production two months later clearly indicate that this version was defective in some respect. The second film was produced on 24 September 1897, and it is probably this version which has survived.[10] It was available within a fortnight for retail sale, with two prints being sold within the first week of October. We should assume that rehearsal was part of this production process, as it was with all his fiction films. A reminiscence connected with the making of a similar film by Robert Paul, *The Sweep and the Whitewasher* of c.1900, offers an account which is relevant to our understanding of the genesis of Smith's film:

> The sweep emerged from the cottage as the whitewasher came up the street, they collided, an altercation followed, the sweep threw soot over the white overalls of the whitewasher, and the whitewasher retaliated by flinging his bucket of whitewash over the sweep. That was the whole story! We rehearsed it once or twice before 'shooting' and Mr Paul gave the three performers a bit of dialogue to help them with the action. Simple dialogue it was – such as 'Ere, where are you going?' 'Look out, clumsy fool...Take that!' 'Oh, you would, would you! Then you take that!'...we only had 40 feet of film to play with then, and the whole thing had to be over in half a minute.[11]

What is the significance of Smith's film? The miller and the sweep express themselves physically, and therefore produce a surprise, a comic moment. To serve the needs of producing this comic effect, they cannot behave as gentlemen, and offer the appropriate courtesies. Smith is providing his audience with recognisable cultural stereotypes who can act violently with little or no provocation. From a position of class prejudice, Smith's characters become contemporary representations of the "vulgar" primitiveness of working-class men. Their actions also facilitate the vicarious pleasure of watching fictional violence. Their fight becomes a conflict for the audience's consumption. This relationship between particular representations of working-class men and their violent interactions within comedy narratives was a feature of the Victorian music-hall, and would develop into an important characteristic of both film comedy and film animation in the next century.

There is an important intertextual explanation for the behaviour of the men in Smith's film. This is found by identifying the film as part of a narrative concept which had a great currency in lantern lectures and on the music-hall stage in Britain from the 1880s. In it, we find a battle between black and white, as represented by either a miller and a sweep, or a whitewasher and a sweep. We can interpret this struggle as a metaphorical argument between opposites. However, the most frequent explanation offered in these "black and white" dramas is that they are fighting for the hand of the same woman. A typical example would be Professor Daltrey and Corporal Higgins' "laughable comic sketch, *The Sweep and the Miller*", which was performed across the country in the early 1880s. The 1883 description for the Brighton Aquarium offers the following account:

> [Daltrey and Higgins] are assisted by Miss Selina Seaforth. The lady artiste personates a buxom housemaid, busy with her domestic duties, when two suitors struck by her charms, appear on the scene. A quarrel ensues, and the lovers agree to decide their little difference by an appeal to arms. Donning the gloves, the sweep and the miller indulge in the manly art in a vigorous and artistic manner...[12]

A lantern reading of twelve slides, entitled *The Miller and the Sweep* (c.1890), used a similar construction:

> But by chance Sam the sweep saw the lovers embrace,
> He forgot his fiancée, grew red in the face,
> And swore a big swear, which I cannot translate,
> That the miller should have a most terrible fate.
> He chased him right into the old linen chest,
> Then closed down the lid, and it must be confessed,
> Lathered him well, as he knelt on the lid,
> Till his arms really ached – serve him right if they did.[13]

The lantern lecture for ten slides from the early 1890s, *The Miller and the Sweep* by F Grove Palmer, offered another version of the story. It dispensed with the romantic interest and, in doing so, provided Smith with an important model for his own interpretation of the story. It began in the following manner:

> Gone, gone was the night
> And the morning was bright,
> The church clock was striking eight;
> When, appointments to keep,
> A sooty black sweep
> Was driven along by his fate.

On the same day,
From the opposite way,
There came a young man from the mill;
And each on his back
Was wearing a sack,
And whistling – trudged with a will.

But alas and alack
For the white and the black!
As they came into juxtaposition,
The dirty, black sweep,
His arm couldn't keep
From causing a cruel collision.[14]

Their fight rages over five more pages of verse and eight more lantern-slides, concluding with a simple sentiment which parodies the moral tale: "You can't touch a soot bag, and not be defiled".

Smith's film is located in this intertextual context. It does not provide any justification for the initiation of this black and white battle, other than their collision, and offers no conclusion. However, as an expression of a popular narrative concept, the film's audiences in the late-1890s would have been very familiar with previous instances of the tale. In performance, this may well have been cemented through an accompanying oral narration presented on-stage when the film was screened. The film, when placed within this history, can be read as an illustration in a new medium of the core action of a familiar story. What can be perceived as missing elements of the narrative in Smith's film are found through an understanding of the other expressions of the tale.

Film versions of *The Miller and the Sweep* would not come to an end with Smith's film. In 1898, he would produce *The Baker and the Sweep*, which the catalogue describes as: "Another comic soot and flour contest. Street scene".[15] The film has not survived, but the description clearly signifies its close affinity with the earlier film. R W Paul, also in 1898, would produce a version of the story, but one with a more intricate narrative construction which revealed very clear character motivations:

A pretty girl is flirting with a sweep, who is busy at his work, but leaves it to assist her. They are observed kissing by her father, the miller, who looks through window. He kicks the sweep, who smothers him from his soot bag. The miller fetches his bag of flour, and retaliates to such effect that neither is recognisable.[16]

Paul brought to his film a woman, her suitor and her father, thus creating a dynamic for the narrative which makes sense of the black and white fight. Smith's film lacks this need for justification. It is blunt and elemental and offers, in itself, no justification for the struggle. In doing so, Smith provides us with the problematical pleasure of viewing male violence.

Comic Face

In medium shot we are presented Tom Green's grotesque features as he drinks and pulls faces for the camera. This "facial", which was made on 28 September at a cost of seven shillings and sixpence for Green's services, epitomises a predominant characteristic of Smith's comic narratives:[17] the desire to challenge the conventional and the respectable. As the first British film comedian, Tom Green appears in this film to revel in being thoroughly naughty. This is an important and essential part of Smith's comic vocabulary. When exhibited as part of a sequence of comic films made by Smith, *Comic Face* would instantly capture the mood of this work. This is a celebration of irreverence and anarchy. Elsewhere in this volume, Garrett Monaghan also associates this film within Bakhtin's understanding of the exaggeration and excessiveness of the body as found in the Rabelaisian world. Smith's comic films would evolve over the next six years, culminating in *Mary Jane's Mishap* of 1903. This essay forms the first part of that wider study.

Notes

As this essay was being completed in July 1999, I learned of the discovery by the NFTVA of a print of the film *The X Rays*. This film is an important addition to Smith's surviving work of 1897, and will offer further insights into Smith's comic world and the development of comic narrative in early British cinema.

[1]   This film list and the catalogue descriptions are drawn from John Barnes, *The Rise of the Cinema in Gt. Britain* (London: Bishopsgate Press, 1983): 234-235. This was the first book to examine Smith's work in 1897. The surviving prints are in the collection of the NFTVA.

[2]   Stop-motion enabled the filmmaker to enter easily into the world of magic. Keeping the camera in a fixed position, a scene is filmed, then the camera is stopped, the scene is changed, and filming is resumed. Stop-motion enabled objects either to disappear or to reappear, or to acquire new characteristics.

[3]   Barnes: 208, from the reference to the film found in Smith's cash book (formerly at the Museum of the Moving Image, London) and reprinted in Barnes.

[4]   "The Brighton Aquarium", *Brighton Herald* 29 September 1894: 3.

[5]   Barnes: 208.

[6]   *Sussex Daily News* 16 February 1897: 2.

[7]   *Warwick Trading Company Catalogue* (London, 1900): 130.

[8]   Barnes: 91.

[9]   Ibid: 206.

[10]   Ibid: 208.

[11]   "The Movie Stars of Muswell Hill", *Evening News* 1 October 1929. Found as a single photocopied page within the Robert Paul section of the Archives of the Barnes Collection, this is an interview with Frank Mottershaw, Paul's assistant. The original page number is missing.

[12]   Letter to the Brighton Aquarium from Daltrey and Higgins, 25 April 1883, in the collection of Hove Museum and Art Gallery.

[13]   "The Miller and the Sweep", in *Lantern Readings, Miscellaneous Tales No. 1* (c. 1890): 4-5. Source: David Henry Collection, British Film Institute Library.

[14]   F Grove Palmer, *The Miller and the Sweep*. Source: Lester Smith Collection, London.

[15]   John Barnes, *Pioneers of the British Film* (London: Bishopsgate Press, 1988): 190.

[16]   Ibid: 180.

[17]   Barnes (1983): 208.

Performing the Passions: Comic Themes in the Films of George Albert Smith

Garrett Monaghan

This essay explores two of the comic motifs in the films of George Albert Smith. Initially, I discuss the relationship between Bakhtin's theory of "grotesque realism"[1] and those films of Smith's which are categorised as "facials". I then consider how the foregrounding of human biological functions resonates in a number of Smith's other films, which focus on female decorum and the misdeeds of servants and maids.

I take the view that the extratextual knowledge required for the construction of meaning and closure[2] in the first decade of filmmaking signalled more than a minimal closure to the early audience. I argue that our task is incomplete while the Victorian spectator is positioned as a naïve consumer, when so many other cultural forms, from popular science lectures and spectacular Dioramas to the theatre, from illustrated novels to the comic strip, presented complex visual narratives to a mass audience.

During the 1880s and 1890s, Smith was a professional producer of illustrated science lectures and Dioramas. From 1882, he was employed by the Society for Psychical Research (SPR), with whom he pursued investigations into the validity of the esoteric pseudo sciences which had derived from Newtonian theories of magnetism and the aether. After this employment, which ended in some scandal,[3] he became – with his wife, the actress Laura Bayley – the leaseholder of St Ann's Well pleasure garden in Hove, adjacent to the seaside resort of Brighton. Here, the Smiths' commercial interests encompassed spectacular entertainments, pageants, photography and filmmaking. The films that emerged from the pleasure garden reworked comic strips, theatrical comedies, music-hall skits, pantomimes and melodrama. For example, *Ally Sloper* (1898) derives from Charles Ross' cartoon character of the same name, the cross-dressing theme of this adventure epitomising the shift from the science of Smith's earlier lectures.

Smith's collaboration with professional actors and actresses, an entourage which included Tom and Nellie Green, Mr Hunter, Laura Bayley and her sisters, suggests that the tools used to design the St Ann's Well films were not located solely in the field of Smith's innovative editorial strategies, and reinforces the need to understand the film-texts as embedded in their historical context. I should note here that, with the lost films, it is necessary to rely upon Smith's catalogue descriptions to identify their content.[4]

Facial expression and bodily functions

Although it was waning towards the end of the 19th century, the established style of British stage acting had sought to play out the inner body, its mental landscape, to "perform the passions".[5] As Professor Moses True Brown had claimed in 1886, acting was a "semiotics" of expressive symbolic gestures and grimaces, a mechanics which signified "the appropriation of the sign to the idea. Give the sign and you suggest the mood."[6]

As the principles of physiognomy, which had also been a subject of research for the SPR, increasingly intersected with theatre performance, facial expressions and distortions supposedly revealed relationships between the visible body and the inner self or theatrical character.[7] I argue that the theatrical stances and facial contortions of pain, ecstasy, grief and surprise trace connections with the distortions of the grotesque body. These exaggerations were also employed in graphic arts to produce humorous illustrations from Leonardo da Vinci's grotesque heads to "The Effect of the Visit of Mr. Dan Leno and Mr. Herbert Campbell to the Houses of Parliament. – No. 2".[8]

19th-century caricature not only relied upon a narrative coherence in the manner of a stereotype, but also supplied the concept of a distorted world – a dream world.[9] In Rodolphe Töpffer's cartoon strips, comically grotesque characters displayed themes that surfaced in the first films. *Le Docteur Festus* (1840) included stories in which scientists "were hurled into outer space by an explosion while their telescope was transported on a steamer",[10] as well as the tale of a grotesque miller dishing out a beating, although not to the sweep, as in Smith's *The Miller and the Sweep* (1897).

The missing terms of the grotesque body, which also populates Victorian fairgrounds, are those of the ideal body and its behaviour. The grotesque body emerges from Bakhtin's work as an incompatible, anticlassical opposition to the humanist ideal of the Renaissance body. By way of an example, an article and illustration on the value of physiognomy in Cassell's *New Popular Educator* (1890) map the hypothetical life of a man from childhood to old age. This illustration, also released as a poster, had considerable cultural currency, being one that was singled out as an example of an important design by M H Spielmann.[11]

The illustration poses class differences as a matter of choice – the poor and ne'er-do-well are depicted with exaggerated countenance, posture and costume. The text claims that "no one can deny that the 'human face' divine has in it something expressive of that which enters into and constitutes the character of the man. It may come out in the eye, or the lip, or the nose, or the general contour of the countenance."[12] The potential which the grotesque bodily exaggerations reasserted for those depicted in the lower half of the artwork was that of a latent degradation. As such, it was a reminder to all spectators of what they held in common, their bodily functions and the cycle of life and death.[13]

In Cassell's poster, the eyes of the resolute, ideal individual are also materially linked to the past and the future, but they look out, straight ahead, along the line of their life, while those of the lower strata are turned down. Bakhtin has argued that the grotesque eye, as opposed to looking straight out as an expression of an individual, self-sufficient human life, turns, protrudes, squints, crosses and rolls, all in a muscular disfigurement of the face. This echoes the convulsions of pain and pleasure, products of a collective flesh, a universal biology that undermined the Renaissance ideals of a conscious, autonomous and individual identity. Thus, what were increasingly relegated to private spheres were bodily functions.

Images that brought those private spheres into a public domain created a tension between the hegemonic constituencies of the private and the public. The framing of film facials, which partitioned the body from the head, also reflected that aspect of the grotesque that sought gratification in the fragmented, fetishised body. Thus, the grotesque head often foregrounds the nose, eyes or mouth, and I am particularly reminded of Williamson's *The Big Swallow* (1901), in which the absent term of this grotesque consumption is excretion. In this kind of humour, the visual signs of facial expression call up synaesthetic associations with the biological body, connecting sight with other sensory modes of perception, for example, where the sight of something calls up the memory of smells or tastes.[14]

Comic Face (A Man Drinking) (Smith, 1897) signals the survival of this grotesque body on the screen, tracing material connections between the humour of the contorted face and the bodily euphoria of drunkenness, or in the pleasurable pain experienced by a woman inhaling snuff (although this second scene has been lost from the extant print).

Licentiousness and drunkenness go together in the popular imagination of Cassell's *New Popular Educator* in a way which invests *Comic Face* with a dialogue between the spectator's extratextual knowledge about social decorum and that part of their biological sense of identity which concerned itself with life as material and the body as matter. The drinker is merry, exaggerating his guzzling and lip-smacking, and holding up his glass in an invitation to join in his feast of oral consumption.

The grotesque banquet locates the acts of eating and drinking within the theme of becoming; what dies is consumed and is excreted. The mouth is part of a collective whole, an orifice which takes the world into its body and thus must excrete it, making the absent term of the mouth the anus.[15] The physical act of consumption transforms the death of what is consumed into a function of birth, a cycle which has no completion. This is a theme which Smith echoes in *The End of All Things* (1897), and Smith's catalogue explains that all manner of things are made merely matter by the mincer, and, as sausages, they are ready to be consumed again. The cycle of consumption and excretion is also played out in *The Hungry Countryman* (1899), but is reversed, the man regurgitating his sandwiches for the spectators' amusement. It is through such liberations from etiquette and decency that grotesque realism invests this humour with political significance, identifying the jest with a popular voice which is positioned as oppositional, radical and subversive, like a *Punch* caricature.

One might read Smith's facials as merely an experiment in new potentials for the screen actor, who must achieve theatrical expression with less vigorous movements than those of the stage actor. This is of some significance because these films were performed by professional stage actors, but this calls up a second consideration. Alongside the rise of a new naturalism in the theatre, there was also the increasing use of props to indicate motivation.[16] If this is compared with the experiments of physiognomists,[17] we discover that facial expression is not easily identified without some further clue. The contortions of pain and ecstasy might easily be mistaken for each other without some form of titling. While such titles are usually present in graphic illustrations, onscreen titles had not surfaced in early films.[18] Thus, not only the actual title of the film – for example, *A Bad Cigar* (Smith, 1900) – but also the use of props signals the intended meanings. The beer bottle, the snuff, the cigar, the Valentine card and the pornographic photograph leave the spectator in no doubt as to the meaning of the expressions.

The use of titling props might be no more than we would expect from professional actors, but this begs the question of choice of prop or scene. In the bourgeois Victorian world, the grotesque body was a central term in defining the private sphere where it dressed, slept, washed, procreated, ate, excreted or worked were all private spaces. The synaesthetic connections opened up by the scopic pleasure of invading these places signalled to spectators, through their biological collectivity, that they were embodied watchers, and, by acknowledging these acts of voyeurism, Smith's comedies dislocated the tensions between the private and public, imbricating contemporary debates about etiquette and decency.

Maids and maidens

Victorian decorum was in a state of siege towards the end of this period. A new order of workers was emerging, one with an increasing disposable income, and liberal tendencies within Socialist and bohemian movements had gone as far as to advocate "free love".[19] If this was the moral code espoused by an élite minority, the new woman was a more widely recognised figure in the street, the home and the press. What might happen if women, whose social actions did not conform to good behaviour, started taking over male institutions, invading the spaces of male privacy, places of shared values and male vulnerability?

If Smith's catalogues can be trusted as a reliable description of his films – and the surviving prints seem to bear this out – *Suffragette in the Barber Shop* (1898) describes the havoc wreaked by the woman who usurps the law of such a space. Here the humour brings about a temporary carnivalesque inversion of male order, admonishing those who would allow such things to happen.

In part, the new woman posed a threat through the public acknowledgment of her status as female flesh, her carnality. Whether or not we now concur with Henry Havelock Ellis,[20] I would argue that his sincere research into the private domain of the eroticised body did reflect the beliefs of the day, and thus of many spectators. In his study of auto-erotism, for example, Ellis gave accounts of how "both in men and women the vibratory motion of a railway-train frequently produces a certain degree of sexual excitement, especially when sitting forward".[21] It is too easy for the 21st-century spectator to see the action of *The Kiss in the Tunnel* (1899) as mild titillation; today, however, the events of the film would still be recognised as a sexual crime.

At the end of the 19th century, the idea of travelling by train was still thought a dangerous activity, at least for a woman travelling alone. Such fears underpinned the theme of many stories such as "Raped on the Railway", published in 1894,[22] or "A Horrible Fright", which describes the plight of the evocatively named Virginia who finds herself trapped in a carriage:

> 'Now, look here,' said the man. 'I know you are frightened...You are alone in a railway carriage with a man who could strangle you and throw your dead body on the line if he felt the least inclined to do so. No no – you don't get the alarm bell. I am keeping guard over that. Now, I may as well tell you frankly that I have come into this railway carriage on purpose to have the pleasure of your society'.[23]

For Smith's local audience in Brighton and Hove, the film must also have resonated with the actual rapes of women on the London-to-Brighton train which had been reported in the local press. The implication of the word "tunnel" in the title is that the actions take place under the cover of darkness – carriage lamps usually blowing out in the wind of a tunnel. Privacy is restored by darkness, blurring the boundaries of the private and the public. This, in turn, offers a reflexive tryst with the spectator's position as one who is watching the illuminated actors from the darkened auditorium.

Part of the pleasure provided is that the characters are performing as if they believe they are in private; thus, the spectator has caught them in the act, and is virtually present, spying on them. The film is further complicated by the apparent complicity of the woman who does not display her contempt for being

27

accosted, but appears to be flattered by the attack, her public sexuality stirring men to uncontrollable passions. Much of this theme, which acknowledges the scopic pleasures of voyeurism and exhibitionism, is reiterated in *As Seen Through a Telescope* (1900).

In this film, the vignetted framing of the fragmentary view-point, or close shot, shifts visual attention from an older male watcher to a bundle of fetish objects – the shoes, laces, stockings, petticoats, ankle and calf of a young woman. As the young woman raises her leg and skirt to place her foot on a bicycle, she is set apart from correct behaviour. The contemporary significance of lifting the foot to tie up the shoelace can be demonstrated by a photostory, "The Man Girl". This story sets the trials and tribulations of a female cross-dresser to a humorous style, in one scene also concentrating on the tying up of bootlaces: "To fasten her boot-string with her foot elevated to the dressing-table is the pride of her life, but it often ends disastrously. Somehow she finds it not so easy to keep her balance as in the old fashion, for sitting on the floor is the real 'girl' way."[24]

Underlying this passage is the notion that rejecting the "real 'girl' way" breaks the ties that bond this woman to heterosexual male notions of correct behaviour. Harry Parkinson's 1898 poster also exploits the erotic capital of the exposed female ankle for Dawson's *The Safety Skirt Holder*.[25] In its juxtaposition, the woman cyclist, who lacks this modesty tool, is shown with her skirt flying up, revealing her ankle boots and bare calf.

Apart from numerous cartoons and short stories ridiculing women wearing cycling trousers, Havelock Ellis also cites cycling as a form of auto-erotism: "I find on inquiry that with the old-fashioned saddle, with an elevated peak rising toward the pubes, a certain degree of sexual excitement, not usually producing the orgasm (but, as one lady expressed it, making one feel quite ready for it), is fairly common among women".[26] The moral indignation about women using their bodies to engage in physical exertion for pleasure was still in currency, and it does not seem unreasonable to suggest that here the saddle and pedals also have further functions as metaphors.

In this short comedy, the bodily freedoms sought out by the new woman appear to be reclaimed through the humour of a threatened, older male order. In the final scene, the young man pushes the old voyeur to the ground and the couple go their separate ways. This action confirms the couple's knowledge of being watched, signalling the brazenness of an emerging new social order in which the woman has been complicit in this public display of the erotic.

This is a doubled exchange in which the old professor's punishment reminds the spectator that they have also been engaged in publicly watching an erotic act. The possibly unintended ironic subversion of Smith's film and Parkinson's poster is that the taboo object is made publicly visible. This opens up alternate and sympathetic counter-readings for the early spectator, in which those who might be outraged by such scenes could be positioned as ridiculous, for the new woman was watching films and riding her bicycle regardless of criticism.

Men's fantasies are also the subject of *Two Old Sports* (1900), in which photographs are ogled and discussed. The film opens with a double-page spread of a racily clad actress, occupying almost half the screen. When the men turn the magazine to look at this picture – if we remember that these were actors (Hunter and Green) well-known to Brighton audiences, who may have been alluding to private knowledge of actresses – the lewd expressions are invested with a deeper significance.

The same theme is taken further in *Where Did You Get It?* (1900), in which the subject of the two old sports' attention is a "naughty" photograph. It would be difficult to speculate on how *naughty* this might have been, without an extant print having yet been found, but it does not seem unreasonable to assume that the photograph contained nudity or actions which would still be considered part of the pornographic image today. The sheer number of surviving pornographic photographs from the time, many of which focused on spanking, suggests that they were generally accessible. Indeed, the catalogue description for *Weary Willie* (1897), which signals that a sado-masochistic fantasy has been transmuted into farce, draws attention to the humorous spectacle of a woman being spanked with a carpet-beater.

Victorian guides to etiquette and social behaviour, such as *The Daughters of England* (1845),[27] make it clear that servants should not be seen or heard, especially if they are engaged in physical, bodily work. The domestic space was understood to be private – even more so the space of domestic work. *The Master, the Mistress and the Maid* (also known as *The Maid in the Garden* or *Hanging Out the Clothes* [1897]) is private business-made-public entertainment. The bad behaviour of female servants, or at least their complicity in bad behaviour, is central to the narrative, as it is to *The Policeman, the Cook and the Copper* (1898), in which the wayward cook must hide her illicit suitor in the boiler.

In *Hanging Out the Clothes*, however, one might presume that the contemporary butt of humour was the master for his carelessness in being caught by his wife. The connection between the private place of the servant's workspace and the public space of her virtual presence on the screen is at once outrageous and rebellious. We are presented with the image of a maid who is knowingly and willingly playing around with her master – a bad girl. For the male spectator, there is the enactment of heterosexual desire, the fetishistic imposition of will; however, the physical beating which the mistress gives the master brings about the silencing of the working woman's voice, as she literally moves into the background.

The masochistic pleasures of submission, a major theme in popular fiction, remain undertheorised for the female spectator in this period. As a young woman in service, and in the audience, their male employers are trouble. But this lower-class maid does not conform to the same moral codes as those of her bourgeois mistress. She may aspire to the material benefits of getting a wealthy partner, or the freedom to act as any other woman or man, to mix with whom she pleases; or she may give herself in order to fulfil her own desire, although marriages across the classes were rarely perceived to work.[28]

Let Me Dream Again (1900) approaches these behavioural codes from the position that men are just after a bit of fun, while their wives are drudges who thwart their freedom. Here an older man and a young woman, dressed for a masked ball of the kind which took place in St Ann's Well pleasure gardens, drink and smoke, while flirting excitedly, as a harbinger to the liaison which might be acted out in the privacy of the bedroom. Once this scene is established, the man awakens to find himself at home in bed, but with his wife, who is cast as a grotesque archetype. As the man pulls away with much grimacing, his wife does likewise in an act of mutual rejection.

The domestic space of the bourgeois bedroom was a nether region, as was the kitchen. But the kitchen was also a place of work, in which female servants must transgress the hegemonic image of a lady. Working manually, sweating and getting dirty, they are closer to the grotesque carnal world.

Mary Jane's Mishap (Smith, 1903) is best-known for Laura Bayley's authorial addendum. For the early spectator, to whom this was a familiar stage device, Mary Jane may have been more recognisable as a clumsy Victorian servant girl, not yet a new Edwardian woman. Mary Jane's awkwardness is pitched against her shyness, implied by the body language of her performance; here Laura Bayley is still playing the part of the maid hanging out the clothes. The character is further complicated by the discovery that her apparent vulnerability is merely a coquettish mask.

Mary Jane seems to revel in her dirt. As she bends to light the range, she draws attention to her bum, which she protrudes, wriggles and scratches, and she is amused by the shoe-polish inadvertently smeared on her face, searching out a mirror to explore the fantasy of a male moustache. The relationship between Mary Jane's dishevelled and dirty face and the gaze of the spectator also resonates with Arthur Munby's photographs of Hannah Cullwick, taken between 1854 and 1900. Hannah was a lower servant whom Munby frequently photographed "in her dirt".[29] Thus, the implied vulnerability of the dishevelled woman in Mary Jane makes a connection with Cullwick, in that their dirt is a sign of their occupation. As Carol Mavor points out,[30] the sight of a dirty servant was an outrage to the sensibilities of employers, sensibilities which are challenged by the public address of this film.

If Mary Jane's lack of scientific knowledge does not allow her fully to comprehend the dangers of using paraffin to light the fire, her lack of knowledge is also commensurate with her status as a woman and a servant. Mary Jane's shyness is also merely a come-on – she is flighty and flirtatious. She is inviting punishment and public censure. If her complicity in this is in any doubt at the moment when her carelessness is at its height, she confronts the spectator in a salacious direct address. Her action is not to point at the word "paraffin" on the can, but, in the medium-close shot, to wink, an authorial intervention which joins the actress Laura Bayley to the spectator and separates her from the character Mary Jane. The outrageous Mary Jane is, of course, duly dispatched to an untimely grave when she is blown literally to pieces.

The description of Mary Jane in the catalogue draws attention to this being a complex story, and makes the point that a lady is seen at the end of the film pointing out the miscreant's grave to her "slaveys" (domestic maids of all work). Although this marks an important use of ellipsis, the servant's body parts have been collected and buried, and the tombstone is in place, which indicates the passage of some weeks; it also confirms the ideological references to notions of ideal female behaviour in the inscription.

This might have left little room for a counter-reading were it not for Mary Jane's return from the grave. Her ghost frightens off the lady and the young servant girls in a move which, whether inadvertently or not, shifts the lady's presence to that of a metaphorical ghost of past and waning ideals. From the point of view of the local audience, this may have had an even greater significance. Mary Jane is a woman who continues to exert influence from beyond the grave and, as such, she is a revenant.

The actions of revenants cross over with religious understandings of dream-sleep, which, for a Brighton audience, must have resonated with the kind of millennial Spiritualism promoted by Robert Owen and Tractarianism, for both had played very significant parts in the cultural life of the locality.[31] This subject, however, is more visible in films other than the comedies, such as *The Gambler's Wife* (Smith, 1899), in which the revenant wife returns from the grave to save her husband from suicide.

I have chosen not to discuss the effect of a public narrator on these films, for I wish to demonstrate their contemporary potential as purely visual narratives, in the light of the audiences' extratextual knowledge. Nor is it possible to come to any neat conclusions about the significance of Smith's work by drawing only on the comic films. The themes, which mark the passage of the extratextual through the St Ann's Well comedies, do not evolve in any smooth chronological order; rather, they appear and reappear through the body of work. Much of what appears to confirm our expectations of Victorian ideological positions is also reversed by the films, connecting them to unexplored, yet contemporary, discourses. Indeed, as I have indicated, the subjects have little to do with Smith's choice of material before his collaboration with Laura Bayley and her professional colleagues, which offers another area of exploration. I suggest, therefore, that we can extend our knowledge by reconsidering the possibility of divergent cultural significances for different audience constituencies, and thereby revisit the unfinished project of understanding these films as part of a newly emerging visual world.

Notes

1   Mikhail Bakhtin, *Rabelais and His World*, translated by Hélène Iswolsky (Cambridge, MA; London: The M.I.T. Press, 1968).

2   Charles Musser, *The Emergence of Cinema: The American Screen to 1907* (New York: Charles Scribner's Sons, 1990).

3   See Janet Oppenheim, *The other world: Spiritualism and psychical research in England, 1850-1914* (Cambridge; London; New York; New Rochelle; Sydney; Melbourne: Cambridge University Press, 1985).

4   *G A Smith Films* (London: Charles Urban Trading Company, 1903).

5   George Taylor, *Players and Performances in the Victorian Theatre* (Manchester; New York: Manchester University Press, 1989): 172.

6   Cited in ibid: 150.

7   See Amy Sargeant, "Darwin, Duchenne, Delsarte", in Linda Fitzsimmons and Sarah Street (eds), *Moving Performance: British Stage and Screen, 1890s-1920s* (Trowbridge: Flicks Books, 2000): 26-43.

8   *Punch, or the London Charivari* 2 April 1902: 249.

9   E H Gombrich, *Art and Illusion: A Study in the Psychology of Pictorial Representation* (Oxford: Phaidon Press, 1960).

10   Ibid: 284.

11   M H Spielmann, "Posters and Poster-Designing in England", *Scribner's Magazine* 18: 6 (1895): 34-47.

12   *New Popular Educator, Volumes One and Two* (London: Cassell, 1890): Volume One: 32.

13   See Lynne Pearce, *Reading Dialogics* (London; New York; Melbourne; Auckland: Edward Arnold, 1994): 57.

14   See Vivian Sobchack, *The Address of the Eye: A Phenomenology of Film Experience* (Princeton, NJ: Princeton University Press, 1992): 75-78.

15   Simon Dentith, *Bakhtinian Thought: An introductory reader* (London; New York; Routledge, 1995): 80.

16   Taylor.

17   See Gombrich: 279-303.

18   An increasing body of evidence suggests that projected titles may well have accompanied many early British film shows, where a second lantern projector was used in conjunction with the film projector, allowing presenters to make up their own titles.

19   See Edward Carpenter, *Love's Coming-of-Age: A Series of Papers on the Relation of the Sexes* (Manchester: Labour Press, 1896).

20   Havelock Ellis, *Studies in the Psychology of Sex, Volume 1: The Evolution of Modesty, The Phenomena of Sexual Periodicity, Auto-Erotism*, third, revised and enlarged edition (Philadelphia: F A Davis Company, 1923).

[21]   Ibid: 176.

[22]   See Patricia Anderson, *When Passion Reigned: Sex and the Victorians* (New York: Harper Collins, 1995): 78.

[23]   L T Meade, "A Horrible Fright", *The Strand Magazine* 8 (July-December 1894): 428.

[24]   "The Man Girl", *Black & White Budget* 4: 57 (10 November 1900): 180.

[25]   Reproduced in Michael Jubb, *Cocoa & Corsets* (London: HMSO, 1984): Plate 75.

[26]   Ellis: 178.

[27]   Mrs Ellis [Sarah Stickney Ellis], *The Daughters of England* (London: Fisher, Son & Co, 1845).

[28]   Judith Rowbotham, *Good Girls Make Good Wives: Guidance for Girls in Victorian Fiction* (Oxford; New York: Basil Blackwell, 1989).

[29]   Cited by Carol Mavor, *Pleasures Taken: Performances of Sexuality and Loss in Victorian Photographs* (Durham, NC; London; Duke University Press, 1995): 73.

[30]   Ibid: 78.

[31]   See John Hawes, *Ritual and Riot* (Lewes: East Sussex County Library, 1995).

The Adventures of the "Vitagraph Girl" in England

Ann-Marie Cook

As part of their publicity campaign to promote the forthcoming trade show of *East is East* (1916), Butcher's Film Service featured advertisements that encouraged exhibitors to book the film because audiences would "immediately feel at home and take delight in recognising British faces, British customs, and British scenes".[1] Curiously, however, the so-called British face that audiences would like best in *East is East* belonged to the *American* actress Florence Turner, and, as she constantly demonstrated in comic films such as *Daisy Doodad's Dial* (1914), it was quite a face indeed. This essay posits that Turner is a critical, although often overlooked, figure at the crossroads of American and British film history. Her extraordinary versatility enabled her to move freely from comedies to dramas, and consolidate her appeal with audiences and critics alike. Perhaps even more fascinating is the fact that Turner's films were cultural hybrids that combined American talent and capital with British talent, themes and locations. Thus, questions arise over whether these were American or British productions. I want to begin by assessing Turner's contribution to British silent comedy. Then I will broaden my investigation to consider the status of her films within British national cinema, because I believe that they have some interesting implications for the way in which we define national cinema and think about the relationship between the British and American film industries.

Florence Turner and the British comedic tradition

The music-hall has been identified as an essential source of inspiration for silent film comedy. Andy Medhurst has noted that "[t]he most important link between cultural modes forged in the halls and the new possibilities of film was, of course, silent comedy...Slapstick film comedy evolved out of [music-hall] sketches...[and] older traditions of mime".[2] The influence of the music-hall on the comedic styles of performers such as Charlie Chaplin and Fred Evans has been well-documented, and I believe that similar connections can be seen in Turner's British comedies. The music-hall influenced Turner's film work by providing a creative incentive for her move to England, and by informing the style and content of her short comedy films. Indeed, in many ways, Turner's work immediately following her arrival in Britain was *defined* by the comic music-hall tradition.

Florence Turner moved to England in 1913 at the height of her fame as the "Vitagraph Girl". As one of America's first true screen "stars", she set out to benefit from her screen success by setting up her own independent production company. In 1919, she told readers of the American magazine *Motion Picture Classics* that she had been forced to move abroad because she could not set up the company in the United States because the Motion Picture Patents Company virtually prevented independent producers from gaining a share in the American market.[3] Citing the success of her films with British audiences and a "faith in the future of the British photo-play",[4] Turner and her producer-manager Larry Trimble established the Turner Films Company at Cecil Hepworth's Walton-on-Thames studio. However, Turner had another compelling reason for leaving the United States. British music-hall managers and booking agents had been so impressed by her New York stage performances that they invited her to come to England. So, instead of making films immediately after her arrival in England, Turner opted to tour the music-hall circuits around the country, following a successful debut at the Pavilion Theatre in Piccadilly Circus on 26 May 1913, and subsequently commenced adapting her American "vaudeville turns" for new audiences.[5] Turner charmed audiences with her "sketches" and impersonations of other popular actors and actresses of the day.[6] Even after Turner began to concentrate on film production, she nevertheless continued to arrange music-hall appearances around her shooting schedule.

Between 1913 and 1914, Turner starred in nine comic shorts: *The Lucky Stone* (1913), *The Younger Sister* (1913), *Creatures of Habit* (1914), *Flotilla the Flirt* (1914), *Daisy Doodad's Dial, Polly's Progress* (1914), *One Thing After Another* (1914), *Film Favourites* (1914) and *Snobs* (1914).[7] *Daisy Doodad's Dial* and *Film Favourites*, in particular, can be seen as cinematic incarnations of the general music-hall tradition and Turner's own unique "turns". *Daisy Doodad's Dial* draws upon the mime tradition by featuring several sequences of close-ups of Turner making hilariously horrifying faces for the camera.[8] While the film attempts to integrate the actress' face-pulling prowess into the framework of a plot, Turner ultimately breaks free of the confines of the narrative by mugging directly to the camera without any apparent narrative motivation. Like her pantomimes and monologues in the music-halls, Turner plays to the spectator, rather than to fellow actors on the set. The emphasis shifts from narrative development to the spectacle of Turner's outrageous faces. Similarly, according to Denis Gifford's description, *Film Favourites* draws upon Turner's legendary music-hall impersonations of leading actors and actresses by casting Turner as a maid who dreams that she is a "'Pathe' heroine, 'Biograph' blonde, Ford Sterling, Sarah Bernhardt, Mabel Normand, and Wild West Billy".[9] This formula proved so successful, in fact, that it was remade in 1924 under the direction of Cecil Hepworth, with Turner impersonating such screen stars as William S Hart, Larry Semon, Mae Murray, Richard Barthelmess and Chaplin.[10] Despite Turner's expressive facial features and comic touch, she seemed virtually to disappear from the comedy scene as a result of her preference for "serious parts".[11] Comedies represent only about one third of Turner's work in Britain, with the remainder of her films falling into the categories of drama, crime and historical romance.[12] Yet, some of Turner's dramatic feature films retain a hint of the music-hall tendencies that shaped her short comedies. The song film *My Old Dutch* (1915) drew upon an actual music-hall song, while the "rags to riches" narrative of *East is East* enabled Turner to turn her hand to a bit of light comedy.

In many ways, Turner's work between 1913 and 1916 marked the last great phase in her career. Following her success in comedy, Turner undertook more ambitious projects, including seven features made between 1915 and 1916.[13] However, as the economic effects of the First World War took their toll on the British film sector, in 1916 Turner and Trimble were forced to return to the United States for business reasons. Although the Ideal Company, which had distributed Turner Films, invited them to return in 1918, the offer was not accepted, leaving what Rachael Low describes as "a noticeable gap in British film production".[14] Turner did return to England briefly to appear in eleven films during the early

1920s, but her career was beginning to decline in the United States. She increasingly found herself playing supportive, matronly roles that seemed far removed from the comic ingénues she had played previously. Nevertheless, Turner's films clearly illustrate the importance of the music-hall in shaping the style of silent film comedy. Turner's performances on the music-hall circuit may have lacked the virtuosity of Chaplin, Fred Evans, Lupino Lane and other silent comedians who made the transition from the "halls" to the screen. Her deliberate clowning to the camera in *Daisy Doodad's Dial* and mimed impersonations of leading entertainment figures in *Film Favourites* should be understood as evidence of a certain tendency within British comedy which drew liberally upon the themes and techniques associated with music-hall humour.

Turner and British national cinema

Turner's British films, both comic and dramatic, remain part of the legacy of American contributions to the formation of British national cinema. Yet, their implications for the question of British national cinema have yet to be thoroughly examined and evaluated. There is no single definition of national cinema, but Andrew Higson has identified four potential strategies for approaching this nebulous concept.[15] It is possible to define national cinema on the basis of industrial factors such as ownership, ability to sustain a national workforce, penetration of foreign markets, and resistance to foreign penetration at home. Alternatively, one might look at whether marketing strategies play upon audience expectations regarding cultural specificity as a brand name to sell the films. Another possibility is to examine exhibition and reception in order to determine which films were being watched, and whether audiences preferred films made at home to those produced abroad. Finally, it is possible to define national cinema on the basis of whether the representational dynamics of films depict attitudes, ideas, traditions and images commonly associated with constructions of national identity. These categories offer a productive basis of inquiry, and I will use them as a framework for my examination of the adventures of the "Vitagraph Girl" in England.

Industrial origins

Beginning with the industrial approach, it becomes evident that the American origins of these films render it difficult to determine their nationality from an economic perspective. The Turner Films Company was owned and operated by Americans following its establishment with capital acquired during Turner's Vitagraph years. Larry Trimble served as production chief, Turner starred as the leading lady, and the American actor Tom Powers was Turner's frequent co-star. However, the films themselves were made in Britain and employed British talent. The most noteworthy British talent at the company was Henry Edwards, a Hepworth player who had been recruited initially to serve as a leading man, but he soon found himself also writing scripts and directing. The films were distributed on both sides of the Atlantic, with Ideal managing British distribution and Mutual handling American bookings. Therefore, it is unclear whether Turner's films are examples of American penetration of the British film market, or British penetration of the American film market. This ambiguity renders it rather difficult to assess the industrial importance of Turner's work within a national cinema paradigm.

Cultural specificity

Despite these ambiguous industrial origins, Butcher's Film Service promoted

Turner's films as "all-British" features, using their cultural specificity as a form of brand name. The *East is East* promotion played on audience recognition of British players such as Henry Edwards and Edith Evans, customs associated with hop-picking and fish-and-chips dinners, and settings such as east London and rural Kent. Another Butcher's Film Service advertisement confirmed the brand name quality of cultural specificity by promising that films worthy of the British name were "[s]trong human life dramas without crude sensationalism. Clean, healthy comedy and charming love stories...built up on British sentiment and ideas".[16] These promotions also played upon the association of Turner's films with other players and films that audiences would recognise as unambiguously British. Indeed, by placing her alongside some of the most famously English players at that time, Butcher's effectively downplayed her American identity. I believe these examples illustrate how publicity established the particular qualities one should expect from an "all-British film". Thus, advertisements for individual films, such as the one for *A Welsh Singer* (1915), did not need to refer to specific themes or scenes because the mere use of Butcher's famous "all-British film" catch-phrase invoked expectations of the culturally specific themes consistently emphasised in their publicity campaigns.[17]

Exhibition and consumption

Booking records published regularly in *The Bioscope*, articles and reviews all indicate that Turner's films were among the most popular productions of their day. *Alone in London* was Ideal's second most popular film in January 1916 (falling narrowly behind *Florence Nightingale*), at a time when other Ideal films on offer included *From Shop Girl to Duchess*, *The Bottle*, *Her Nameless (?) Child* (1915), *The Enemies* and *The Mystery of Edwin Drood*.[18] By November of that year, *A Welsh Singer* would score a record-breaking 800 bookings, making it the most popular Ideal release at the time.[19] This popularity cannot measure Britishness, but it proves that audiences favoured Turner's work just as much as productions without American connections. One could argue, however, that audience response provides a measure of how authentic the film's depiction of English settings and lifestyles really was; and the success of Turner's films suggests that British audiences appreciated their representation of national identity. As for American exhibition, I have not yet uncovered Mutual's booking records, but the limited coverage of reviews and publicity suggests that Turner's films were not as popular as films produced at home without foreign involvement.

Perhaps one reason for Turner's extraordinary popularity, which seemed to transcend the usual appeal of American players, was that she actively embraced British culture in a way that other actors and actresses did not. She toured England, Scotland and Wales, shooting films on location (using locals as extras), endearing herself to the public with press interviews in which she expressed her love for all things British, and appearing in music-halls and theatres around the country.[20] In return, the willingness of the audience and the film industry in general to adopt her as one of their own seemed to generate an aura of populism around her persona. In fact, the publicity surrounding Turner deliberately downplayed her American roots by framing her as a product of British culture. Descriptions of her background proclaimed that she was related to the great English landscape painter J W M Turner.[21] Meanwhile, *Illustrated Film Monthly* noted a trace of the "West Scotland Celt" in Turner's dark features, and attributed it to the fact that her "grandparents were of stock and born in Scotland".[22] This tendency to obscure Turner's true nationality and portray her as a "local" talent represents a fascinating twist in the question of national cinema.

Although Turner Films was founded with American capital, it generated profits for the British industry with films that did not appear to inspire the cultural anxieties which American films would subsequently arouse. On the contrary, *The Bioscope* praised *My Old Dutch* as "an achievement of unique importance in the field of British cinematography".[23] The trade publication also applauded *East is East* for its depiction of London cockney life and familiar English settings, complimenting Turner and Henry Edwards for "appear[ing] to very great advantage in characters which cannot fail to commend themselves to the sympathies of a British audience".[24] These reviews exemplify the complimentary tone that usually characterised assessments of Turner's contribution to British cinema.[25]

Although American reviews consistently recognised these films as British, there was disagreement over whether this Britishness lent them charm or rendered them unworthy of American audiences. One possible reason for this negativity could be the lack of an active campaign by the Mutual company to promote the American release of these films. In fact, a representative from Mutual admitted to *Variety* that the company elected to release *Far From the Madding Crowd* (1915) first because it was the weakest of all the features.[26] With such publicity, it is hardly surprising that *The New York Times* did not even bother to review any of them, and that *Variety* itself reviewed only five, completely ignoring *Doorsteps* (1916) and *Lost and Won* (1915).

Critics generally approved of the "realistic" depictions of British settings, but had little patience for what they considered conventional and class-bound narratives presented with unimaginative style. In its review of *Far From the Madding Crowd*, *Variety* complained that Turner lacked the physical characteristics to portray simple ingénues convincingly, and that the pacing of the film was so foreign in style that American audiences would not be able to follow it. The review concluded that the film's general atmosphere resembled that of stories which "appeared a decade to two ago in 'The Fireside Companion,' intended primarily for consumption in the scullery and pantry by the maids and the cook".[27] *Alone in London* fared slightly better, earning the reluctant recommendation that Turner's performance would make the film "satisfactory" for American audiences. Nevertheless, it was still declared so "hopelessly old fashioned that the acting, stage direction, and photography are all that could possibly be contributed to the unfolding of so conventional a tale".[28] *A Welsh Singer* earned praise for being "better by far than...the first of the Turner series", although such comparison to the much-loathed *Far From the Madding Crowd* blunts the compliment considerably.[29] Only *My Old Dutch* earned the glowing commendation that the "rigid adherence to detail in depicting coster life contributes in no small measure to the general effect of this wonderful five-part feature".[30] One can only wonder why the Britishness of this film did not generate the criticism that the other features did, and the review itself seems quite oblivious to this glaring inconsistency. However, the overall response to Turner's films was that they were too predictable and old-fashioned, too slow in their pacing, too static in their framing, too primitive in style, and too seeped in Englishness to attract a wide American audience.

Representation

Clearly, therefore, references to Britishness and Englishness crop up repeatedly in the promotion and reception of these films, and I will build my analysis around what I see as the four main cultural/national representational dynamics. Firstly, Turner's films reflected a geographically accurate version of Britishness. It is commonly accepted that the British label refers to something which is applicable primarily to England, Scotland and Wales; Turner's films can be seen as conforming to this model because she did not restrict her work to England. She filmed on location in Scotland and Wales, and performed in regional theatres and music-halls in her free time.[31] Reviews also noted the authenticity that such regional locations brought to the films. *The Bioscope* went so far as to suggest that *A Welsh Singer* presented "a vivid and accurate picture of rural life".[32] Instead of retaining an Anglo bias, Turner's films depicted a geographically integrated Britishness.

Secondly, Turner also approached Englishness from a slightly unusual vantage by focusing upon working-class experiences, instead of upper-middle-class and aristocratic lifestyles which have often been associated with representations of English identity (especially in Cecil Hepworth's films). By framing the "rags to riches" story in a way that ultimately rejects wealth in favour of a comfortable, rural lifestyle, *East is East* romanticises the working class.[33] As Turner's character, Victoria Vickers, is introduced, intertitles make light of her tattered clothes by humorously referring to her "open work" stockings. Despite their poverty, the film's characters are kind-hearted, high-spirited cockneys, with an appreciation for simple pleasures such as fish-and-chips dinners. With generous spirits that prompt them to lend anything from cigarettes to "tanners", they lead a contented life in London's East End until they find true happiness in the idyllic landscape of Kent. It was precisely this valorisation of simple values and the rural idyll which appealed to British reviewers.

By contrast, *Variety* considered *East is East* "totally unsuited for American audiences, as it is essentially English in its atmosphere". The most objectionable aspects of the film were its coster slang intertitles and a plot that "centered on the premise that...no matter how much money drops on one...the fact remains that East is East and it will never mingle with those that have been reared in the West End".[34] Perhaps the reason why this "English atmosphere" was so unsuitable for Americans was that it reflected attitudes about class which ran contrary to the idea that anyone could overcome poverty to achieve the wealth and success associated with the American Dream. The review appears to rest upon a binary assumption that equates the West End with success, and the East End with failure. Thus, it completely overlooks the cultural significance of Victoria and Bert's move to Kent. Although the American Dream's emphasis on wealth and material possessions leaves little room for appreciating the simplicity of owning a modest cottage in the hop fields, English culture has traditionally prized such rural lifestyles. Moreover, the review similarly disregards the entrepreneurial aspect of Bert Grummit's transformation from an East End "knockabout" to a successful owner-manager of a chain of fish-and-chips shops. It would seem that the film is not nearly as incompatible with the American Dream as *Variety* made it appear. Moreover, with plots that revolved around match girls who become great stage actresses (*Doorsteps*), shepherdesses who become famous singers (*A Welsh Singer*), and common working folk who unexpectedly come into enough money to live comfortably (*East is East* and *My Old Dutch*), Turner's films reflect a surprisingly democratic sensibility and one of wish-fulfilment. Perhaps another reason for Turner's popularity was that her characters were common folk with whom her audience could readily identify. This popularity further suggests that audiences responded favourably to the depiction of British culture in the film.

The third aspect of representation relates to the display of landscape in Turner's films. *East is East* prominently featured Kent's hop fields; *A Welsh Singer* depicted the rugged Welsh countryside; and *My Old Dutch* framed the young couple's courtship against the backdrop of Hampstead Heath. Landscape has often been equated with constructions of national identity, with Cecil Hepworth translating this connection into the language of cinema.[35] But, unlike Hepworth's features, the landscape in Turner's films is dominated by ordinary "backbone of

Britain" folk, which undoubtedly contributed to her populism. The review of *East is East* in *Pictures and the Picturegoer* picks up on this almost classless, utopian quality of the countryside by framing Kent as a deliverance from the East End poverty and West End ostentatiousness that Victoria experiences in the film.[36] Thus, geographic particularity of the landscape together with the general symbolic importance it plays in the national consciousness suggest that rural settings in Turner's films can be seen as indicators of national identity.

Finally, the Britishness of Turner's films can be seen in their representation of the nation's literary, theatrical and music-hall traditions. *East is East, Far From the Madding Crowd* and *A Welsh Singer* were adapted from novels; *Alone in London* and *Doorsteps* had been popular theatre productions; and *My Old Dutch* was inspired by a popular music-hall song. The cultural significance of the music-hall can certainly be seen as giving the "song film" a specific national brand. Moreover, since Turner's films tended to remain faithful to the original play or novel, rather than take artistic liberties with the original text, this approach to film adaptations reflects what Brian McFarlane and Charles Barr have identified as a trade mark of British cinema, since foreign adaptations tended to take more creative liberties with original texts.[37] Finally, it is important to note that these literary and theatrical sources were not the highbrow canonical works that one associates with a "quality cinema" (excluding Hardy's *Far From the Madding Crowd*), and this further contributes to Turner's populism. By taking inspiration from texts that were part of the nation's literary, theatrical and music-hall heritage, Turner's films became part of the British cultural milieu.

Conclusion

Florence Turner may not immediately come to mind when one thinks of music-hall, British silent comedy or even British national cinema, but she has clearly played a significant role in the development of all three. In addition to exemplifying a tendency within British silent comedy to draw upon the music-hall tradition, Turner's films illustrate the importance that exhibition, reception, representation and cultural specificity play in defining the "nationality" of a film. Moreover, Turner's films offer the perfect opportunity to re-evaluate the way we understand the relationship between British and American cinema. Some scholars such as Rachael Low have recognised the positive aspects of the American influence on British filmmaking, but the relationship continues to be characterised overall in primarily negative terms.[38] The harmful effects of the hegemonic association between the two industries cannot be ignored, but neither should they overshadow instances where the American influence energised British national cinema. Perhaps the example of Florence Turner will foster subsequent research that may transform the way in which we think about the relationship between British and American cinema. But for now, let us simply pay tribute to Florence Turner for providing us with extremely popular films that featured British settings and themes, and generated profits on both sides of the Atlantic. British national cinema was made even richer thanks to the adventures of the "Vitagraph Girl" in England!

Notes

I would like to thank Andrew Higson and Jeff Smith for their comments on earlier drafts of this essay, and Fred Lake and Mike Hammond for providing me with fascinating articles on Turner's work.

1   *The Bioscope* 33: 523 (19 October 1916): 228.

2   Andy Medhurst, "Music Hall and British Cinema", in Charles Barr (ed), *All Our Yesterdays: 90 Years of British Cinema* (London: British Film Institute, 1986): 171.

3   Elizabeth Peltret, "The Return of Florence Turner", *Motion Picture Classics* February 1919: 29.

4   *Illustrated Film Monthly* April 1914: 94.

5   Robert Grau, *The Theatre of Science: A Volume of Progress and Achievement in the Motion Picture Indsutry* (London; New York: Benjamin Blom, 1969): 210.

6   "American Players in England", *Moving Picture World* 18 July 1914: 441.

7   See Denis Gifford, *The British Film Catalogue 1895-1985: A Reference Guide* (Newton Abbot; London: David & Charles, 1986). My analysis relies upon Gifford's designation of the films as comedies, dramas, crime and romance. Of these nine titles, only *Daisy Doodad's Dial* exists as a viewable film at the National Film and Television Archive (NFTVA).

8   Film synopsis: Turner and Tom Powers star as husband and wife who enter a face-making contest. The film begins with a close-up of Turner practising for the contest by making various faces directly at the camera. When a toothache prevents Daisy (Turner) from participating in the contest, her husband competes and returns home with a first prize ribbon – much to her chagrin. Daisy enters a second contest, but is arrested for disturbing the peace after she creates a scene in a train carriage by practising her faces. Daisy's husband bails her out of jail, but not in time to compete in the contest. Upon returning home, a disappointed Daisy finds that her dreams are haunted by her own faces, as one zany expression fades into another. The film concludes with a close-up on Turner making a series of faces directly at the camera without any apparent narrative motivation.

9   Gifford: film number 05221.

10   E E Barrett, "Ivor in Bloomsbury", *The Picturegoer* 11: 65 (May 1926): 14.

11   "Picture Personalities: Pithy Paragraphs About People in Pictureland", *Pictures and the Picturegoer* 6: 2 (28 February 1914): 41.

12   See Denis Gifford, *The Illustrated Who's Who in British Films* (London: B T Batsford, 1978): 287-288.

13   *My Old Dutch, Alone in London, Far From the Madding Crowd, Lost and Won, A Welsh Singer, Doorsteps* and *East is East*. Of these titles, only *East is East* exists as a viewable film at the NFTVA.

14   Rachael Low, *The History of the British Film 1914-1918* (London: George Allen & Unwin, 1950): 79.

15   Andrew Higson, *Waving the Flag: Constructing a National Cinema in Britain* (Oxford: Clarendon Press, 1995): 4-6.

16   *The Bioscope* 33: 526 (9 November 1916): 542.

17   *The Bioscope* 30: 491 (9 March 1916): 1016.

18   *The Bioscope* 30: 482 (6 January 1916): 24.

19   *The Bioscope* 33: 528 (23 November 1916): 744.

20   "Editorial", *Pictures and the Picturegoer* 10: 124 (1 July 1916): 277.

21   "Picture Personalities: Pithy Paragraphs About People in Pictureland": 41.

22   *Illustrated Film Monthly* April 1914: 94.

23   "'My Old Dutch.' Mr. Chevalier's Coster Characters", *The Bioscope* 28: 456 (8 July 1915): 169.

24   "A Hop-Picker's Romance", *The Bioscope* 33: 525 (2 November 1916): 431.

25   See also the reviews for *Doorsteps* in "From Servant Girl to Leading Lady", *The Bioscope* 30: 489 (24 February 1916): 858-859, and *A Welsh Singer* in "A Charming Story Told in Beautiful Pictures", *The Bioscope* 478: 29 (9 December 1915): 1165.

26   Fred, "Far From the Madding Crowd", *Variety* 30 June 1916.

27   Ibid.

28   Jolo, "Alone in London", *Variety* 25 June 1915.

29   Fred, "A Welsh Singer", *Variety* 25 August 1916.

30   Jolo, "My Old Dutch", *Variety* 16 July 1915.

31   See "American Players in England" for an account of Turner's participation in a stage production at the same time that she was filming *Through the Valley of Shadows* (1914) on location in south Wales. The article also previews *The Shepherd Lassie of Argyll* (1914), a historical romance filmed on location in Scotland.

32   "A Charming Story Told in Beautiful Pictures": 1165.

33   Plot synopsis: Victoria Vickers lives in Poplar East with her adopted family and her friend, Bert Grummit. While working at picking hops in Kent, Victoria learns that she has inherited a fortune. A stipulation of the inheritance requires her to live with a West End society matron with whom she is expected to learn how to behave like a lady. She uses some of her money to help Bert start his fish and chips business. When her new guardian's son tries to seduce her to get her money in order to pay off gambling debts, Victoria decides that having money is not all it is cracked up to be. In the end, she rejects the upper-class lifestyle in favour of a quiet cottage in Kent with Bert.

34   *Variety* 10 November 1916.

35   For example, see Higson: 26-97 for a discussion of the connection between landscape and identity in the films of Cecil Hepworth. In addition to specific analysis of Hepworth's use of rural locations, Higson also examines some of the key writings on the general cultural significance landscape holds within constructions of English identity.

36   "Right off the Reel", *Pictures and the Picturegoer* 17: 302 (29 November 1919): 635.

37   Charles Barr, "Before *Blackmail*: Silent British Cinema", in Robert Murphy (ed), *The British Cinema Book* (London: British Film Institute, 1997): 5-16; and Brian McFarlane, *Novel To Film: An Introduction to the Theory of Adaptation* (Oxford: Clarendon Press, 1996).

38   See Low for further examples of British filmmakers adopting elements of the American studio system, such as the promotion of individual stars, and the shift from the cottage industry towards a more industrialised structure with specialisation and division of labour.

Trilby (1914):
Theatre to Film

Trish Sheils

This essay will examine the 1914 British film *Trilby* in terms of its cinematic and theatrical qualities. It is organised into three sections: the first two sections deal with the background to Paul Potter's melodramatic stage version of *Trilby* (1895) and its adaptation into film, while the third section focuses on the shifting performance codes during the late-19th and early 20th centuries, and identifies different acting discourses in the film text.

While the film *Trilby* is clearly not a British comedy, its melodramatic qualities allowed the performers, especially Sir Herbert Beerbohm Tree, to draw on traditional comedic conventions to provide dramatic relief from the more intense and spectacular elements of the plot, which I will discuss towards the end of this essay. However, the style of acting that was considered appropriate for the 19th-century stage later began to be overshadowed by a more restrained style which led to the rhetorical codes of melodramatic performances to be considered unrealistic or even comic in their stylised and extravagant gestures. This is evident in the screen version of *Trilby*, as Tree virtually fills centre-frame with his posturing, often playing as much to the audience as to the characters onscreen. He draws us to his large actions as he hides behind a screen to eavesdrop on Trilby and Little Billee, who generally act in a more restrained manner – although, in one highly pictorial scene, we do see Billee facing centre-frame in a stylised melodramatic pose of covering his eyes in despair. In contrast, Tree draws on presentational codes of performance to create a pictorial effect as he jostles out the other more restrained actors and postures broadly in an extravagant style. Indeed, his make-up and hair create a spectacle in themselves, while his facial gestures and exuberant eyes, especially in the closer shots, suggest the magnitude of his personality. He uses his fingers to create a pictorial posture, while his large gestures of hands on hip replicate both Du Maurier's original sketches and many of the publicity photographs for the stage productions. However, this style of acting began to seem absurd, as narrative continuity began to dominate cinematic texts, and theatrical presentational codes were overshadowed by more representational conventions. The increased use of close-ups made the histrionic facial gestures too exaggerated and even grotesque, and the style lent itself to the type of parody that we see in the 1914 film comedy *Daisy Doodad's Dial*.[1] By examining performance codes in more detail, however, I will challenge this notion of melodramatic acting, in both the stage play and the film, as being merely absurd or comic.

Background to the stage and film versions of *Trilby*

The 1914 film *Trilby* was based on Paul Potter's 1895 stage adaptation of George

Du Maurier's novel of the same name. The plot centres on a bohemian Irish orphan, Trilby O'Farrell, who poses as an artist's model in the Latin Quarter of Paris. She befriends three male British student artists, Taffy, the Laird and Little Billee. Taffy and the Laird provide light relief from Little Billee's middle-class Englishness and his sensitive artist's nature, while Trilby defies conventional codes of femininity with her swearing, smoking, unusual dress codes and bare feet. This representation of femininity, however, gradually loses its distinctiveness as she and Little Billee fall in love with each other, and he begins to judge her sexual and social freedom by middle-class norms. Eventually, as in Alexandre Dumas *fils'* novel *La Dame aux Camélias* (1848; produced as a play in 1852), love overcomes class differences and they become engaged. This union, however, is threatened by the arrival of Little Billee's mother and his uncle who plead with Trilby to forego the marriage for the sake of Billee's reputation. Having initially refused Billee on the same grounds, Trilby agrees.

The other, more dramatic, threat to their union is provided by the character of Svengali, a highly gifted Jewish musician who hangs around the Latin Quarter scrounging money. He, too, falls in love with Trilby, but his relationship is bound much more to her unusual voice. While she is musically "tone deaf", he recognises that the timbre of her voice could be trained to make her an accomplished opera singer. Svengali's powers of mesmerism enable him to hypnotise Trilby under the guise of curing her headaches – thus compelling her to write a farewell letter to her fiancé, forcing her acceptance to marry Svengali, and developing her creative talents as a singer. This interest in mesmerism not only reflects the growing fascination in the power of the unconscious during the second half of the 19th century, but also distinguishes the more sinister and spectacular quality of this melodramatic text. There is also a suggestion in the text that Trilby acquiesces to her subliminal creative desires by marrying Svengali, rather than opting for domesticity with Billee in a small English village. Inevitably, compared to Billee, the character of Svengali takes on a much more dramatic colour and magnitude as his portrayal is heightened to diabolic intensity and grotesque comedy through his filthy clothes, greasy and wild hair, unshaven face and exaggerated facial and body gestures.

The plot concludes with the three students returning to Paris five years later to hear Trilby singing in a concert. Svengali's heart is failing under the pressure of continually hypnotising Trilby for her concerts. During this performance, he dies from a heart attack and she is left on-stage singing humiliatingly out of tune. Billee once again declares his love for her, but, before they are about to be married, a portrait of Svengali arrives for her. Drawn to the portrait, Trilby mysteriously calls Svengali's name and follows him to her death as she collapses into the arms of Little Billee. This closure confirms not only the magnetic power of Svengali, which drives the melodramatic trajectory, but also 19th-century melodramatic conventions of death for fallen women who deviate from conventional norms of virtuous femininity.

Paul Potter's stage adaptation, starring the renowned actor/manager Herbert Beerbohm Tree as Svengali, was a great success, and toured both Britain and the United States to popular acclaim. Tree's esteemed reputation as a significant actor of the legitimate stage was greatly enhanced by his role as Svengali, which many considered to be his best part, and his financial success from this production later funded the building of Her Majesty's Theatre in London. The appeal of *Trilby* also extended into the 20th century with the development of cinema permitting further film adaptations of this popular play. Hence, by 1914, Beerbohm Tree was starring once again as Svengali, but this time on celluloid.

As Rachael Low has noted, from 1906 to the beginning of the First World

War the film industry developed considerably as a profession, and during the last four years of this period the legitimate stage considerably influenced this shift.[2] Six British films of Shakespeare's plays were produced between 1906 and 1914, including W G Barker's *Henry VIII* in 1911. This film version relied exclusively upon Beerbohm Tree's stage production for its material, and involved transporting all the actors, sets and properties from Her Majesty's Theatre to film studios in Ealing. In his attempt to draw on the established reputation of the legitimate stage for his film, Barker not only paid Tree £1000 for one day's work, but also aimed simply to replicate the stage production on film.[3] As he stated in the publicity brochure for the film:

> My object in trying to induce Sir Herbert Tree to allow his prodigious success, *King Henry VIII* to be kinematographed was not only to interest, amuse, and educate the myriads of Picture Theatregoers, but also to enable me to hand down to posterity a faithful, silent, and permanent record of the wonderful, life-like portrayal and representation of some of the most important personages and incidents in the eventful history of England.[4]

Harold Shaw's 1914 adaptation of *Trilby* for Dr R T Jupp's London Film Company also relied upon Beerbohm Tree's stage personality to legitimise the film as a respectable form of entertainment. His success is indicated in an article in *The Sunday Times* entitled "The Picture Theatre, Trilby Filmed":

> In the presence of a large and distinguished assembly, including several prominent personalities identified with the legitimate stage, the film version of Trilby, featuring Sir Herbert Beerbohm Tree in his favourite role of Svengali, was presented at the West End cinema, Coventry Street, on Wednesday last. The picture is photographically perfect in every respect, being both clear and well-defined. Trilby must surely be included in the category of photoplay that will live long in the memories of those who view it. The vast audience accorded it a rousing reception.[5]

However, this production drew much more on a cinematic syntax even as it was identified with the stage version. Low suggests that this may be attributed to the fact that Jupp began his company with a healthy capital of £40 000, which allowed him to advertise in the United States for cinematic expertise. Harold Shaw, an American who had been acting in, and directing, films for Edison, was engaged by Jupp in 1913 as one of the principal producers for the London Film Company, and his first film, *House of Temperley*, was released in September 1913 to an immediate success. Other American personnel engaged by Jupp included actress Edna Flugrath, who later married Shaw, and plot writers Anne and Bannister Merwin who also had worked for Edison.[6] Bannister Merwin, in particular, was very much aware of cinema as a distinctive medium, and his reputation was built on his knowledge of the technical possibilities of film. In an interview in *The Bioscope* in April 1914, he stated:

> [A]daptations must always be false...I don't think that they will last much longer, or, at any rate, be nearly so prevalent, when writers realized the possibilities of the cinematograph as a distinct new means of expression.[7]

The cinema plot and the film

The way in which Harold Shaw utilised cinematic discourses for his film adaptation of *Trilby* can be appreciated by first considering the scenario (located in the Beerbohm Tree Collection), and, secondly, by examining how this was transcribed into film. It is worth noting that the extant film material[8] only includes the first act of the play, whereas the scenario deals with the whole play/novel.[9]

The intention of the London Film Company to explore the cinematic possibilities of the new medium while, at the same time, legitimising its theatrical legacy is evident in the planned opening shot of the *Trilby* scenario which reads as follows:

> A. Sir Herbert Tree, without make-up – fade out – fade back – Sir Herbert Tree as Svengali – fade out.

Tree's reputation as an actor on the "legitimate stage" is emphasised by the first shot of him as an actor while his theatrical role as Svengali is highlighted in the second shot. The cutting and the use of fades, however, mark the filmic qualities of this adaptation. The use of sets for the film adaptation also exceeds those used in the stage production, and links the cinematic text much more closely to the pictorialism of Du Maurier's novel with its ability to elide between scenes. For example, proposed film sets include Svengali's room; outside Trilby's lodgings; an exterior street scene; studios A and B, and the hallways outside them; a country road; the interior of an English country home, and a location shot outside a railway station (although a note in brackets adds that "Any Railway Station would do", perhaps suggesting that even pictorial realism had its limits). In the final film, however, we see only the two artists' studios and a studio set of an outside street, and, because the other two acts are missing, it is not possible at this stage to establish what exactly was included in the finished film.[10]

Charles Musser's work on the shifts in narrative structuring of Hollywood films after 1907 suggests that, as the subjects for film narratives expanded, and well-known books and stage plays were adapted, reliance on an audience's textual preknowledge could not necessarily be assumed. One of the strategies to increase narrative clarity was the use of intertitles, which, "because they were an inexpensive and extremely effective way to clarify a narrative, they quickly became standard".[11] The cinema plot for *Trilby*[12] uses extensive intertitles, or subtitles as they are referred to in the plot, but a handwritten note at the beginning of the screenplay states that "those given are not put forward as final forms, but to indicate what is to be conveyed". The final screen version does not use all those proposed, but, like the Hollywood models, included enough to link the cuts efficiently and to smooth over disjunctions in the narrative. However, the structures of melodrama also rely upon tableaux, spectacle and pictorialism, which function to arrest narrative flow for the purpose of theatricality.

A Nicholas Vardac's examination of the "growth of a new realism in staging and acting" indicates an aesthetic link between the pictorial realism of the late-19th-century stage and that of early cinema. In discussing actor-manager David Garrick's staging of plays in the 19th century, Vardac states:

> Garrick's new aesthetic departure...was that of achieving a greater pictorial realism in staging...by the withdrawal of his production into the proscenium picture frame, as well as by changes in lighting and in character interpretation. He was aiming at theatrical production pictorial, thus cinematic, in conception.[13]

This concept of pictorial realism can be examined in the different cinematic and theatrical approaches to visual effects in *Trilby*. In the theatrical production of *Trilby*, when Svengali acknowledges that he can work magic on Trilby, the stage directions draw on colour and lighting to enhance the effect: "It is now dark – red glow from fire. Gas almost out, green lens on Svengali's face."[14] The technical prompt for this,[15] found in the cinema plot in the Beerbohm Tree Collection, also emphasises this pictorial effect:

> Limes and electric lights go down gradually
> CHANGE BACK CLOTH TO MOONLIGHT
> Bring up blue in floats and batten
> Lights going finally down
> Call Trilby
> Bring up Green on Svengali's face.

The theatrical effect of these colour changes creates a sinister effect. However, although limited to black and white photography, the cinema plot's planned approach to cinematography suggests an equally sinister and rather highly cinematic effect using shadows. In Scene 56, in Svengali's room, the cinema plot reads:

> Svengali and Gecko discovered – Svengali goes to window – sunset
> on his face – the shadow gradually rises showing setting of sun –
> sends Gecko off – as the shadow rises to his face he begins to work
> and call for Trilby, Trilby, Trilby.

And, as one final example of the way in which contemporary cinematic description is employed in the planning of the film in 1914, at the end of the plot there is an interesting comment regarding cinematic closure and perceived audience reception:

> The scenes leading to the Finale would be suited to the foregoing
> – and, as nearly as possible, the way Sir Herbert finished the play
> – except that it is advisable to join Billee and Trilby happily –
> since the average *Cinema* audience are not fond of solving
> problems – nor are the average Exhibitors fond of showing films
> that are unsatisfactory to the average audience.

The Bioscope article also comments that the change of a "promise of future happiness for the hero and heroine...will undoubtedly add to its popularity with the public".[16] This suggests that theatre audiences were conceived as more sophisticated than those for the cinema, and supports the view that the theatre legitimised the cinema for more middle-class tastes.

Performance codes

With regard to performance codes, however, cinema and theatre had to appeal to different sections of the audience, and, while some aesthetic conventions favoured a more restrained acting style, often termed (problematically) as "*realist*" in critical discourses, others were drawn to more ostentatious or romantic codes. These differences were, and still are, to some extent, often polarised and associated with specific, approved or disparaged genres. Melodrama, for example, has often been accused of being too stagy and unrealistic by theatre and film critics who generally favoured the more restrained codes of middle-class sensibilities. However, it might be more useful to determine melodrama and "realism" in terms of their relationship to the audience, in that what was considered *realistic* in the theatre usually meant an acknowledgment of the invisible fourth wall, whereby audiences looked on as voyeurs of (mainly representational) dramas in which actors often turned away from the front of the stage. This style of acting developed from the latter half of the 19th century, since the established or presentational codes of 19th-century performance had, up to that point, encouraged a much more direct relationship with the audience. In the presentational code of performance, actors tended to play to the front of the stage, drawing on stylised postures and movement to articulate meaning.

To problematise this tension further, the presentational codes also incorporated different pictorial styles, which Janet Staiger (citing Alan S Downer) usefully summarises when she notes that theatre acting of the early 1800s, which played directly to the audience, could be divided into three groups:

1) The Kemble (or Teapot) School in which the speaker "took a fixed pose, like an ancient statue; body and face gestures were conventional and controlled".

2) The Kean style where the "actor's body position and gestures were those of vigorous action, with occasional violent motions. More face gestures than the Kemble method were used."

3) The Macready method integrated both the Kemble and the Kean styles.[17]

These methods also provided the basic models for melodrama.

The sense of stage frontality and pictorialism inherent in these styles was considered naturalistic at the time. From the mid-19th century, however, these styles shifted to accommodate the more representational methods of acting. By the end of the century, the role of the individual actor was seen as less to "fill the stage" through posturing and stage personality, and rather to offer interpretation of character with the management of stage sets, props and improved lighting satisfying audience demands for pictorial realism. Furthermore, as underplaying character motivation and increased use of staging provided the paradigms for critical discourses, the older and popular methods were frequently disparaged, often on class grounds.

The association of the literati with the representational or *realistic* codes of acting in the theatre also contributed to class distinctions regarding different styles of performance. While melodrama had developed from popular forms of entertainment for the working classes from the end of the 18th century, it had been appropriated by the middle classes by the mid-19th century, and it developed cross-class appeal. However, the reinstating of copyright laws by the mid-19th century also encouraged the literati to return to writing for the stage, and this shifted the emphasis much more onto the text and character, and away from the stage where sensational effects and highly stylised stage performers had created a more rhetorical form of theatre.[18] The representational style of acting that evolved alongside these changes tended to become associated with the legitimate stage, while music-hall and melodrama retained to some extent their links with popular performance codes.

These distinctions, however, are problematic as the appeal of melodrama across the classes still prevailed. Even by July 1913, a London correspondent for the *Dundee Advertiser* noted:

Whatever the reasons may be – and various reasons have been put forward from too much realism to too much rag-time – there can be no doubt that the craving for melodrama is greater than it ever was. What is more, the craving seems to have extended to the more cultural sections of the society.[19]

Tree's use of melodrama in his productions, as well as his referral to more established Shakespearian texts, demonstrated his refusal to conventionalise his approach to drama. His performance in *Trilby*, I would argue, actually drew on different codes of performance, which he used interchangeably. Tree confirmed this to a reporter on the *Glasgow Herald* in October 1896:

> But there was no difference between romance and realism. They were potentially interchangeable. Everything that tended to stimulate the imagination of the audience, he contested, was legitimate on the stage.[20]

This approach was also informed by his attempts to provide a theatre with a cross-class appeal, and he was cited by W L Courtney in reference to the programme of Her Majesty's Theatre: "I have to find something which will be agreeable to stalls, upper circle, pit, gallery – all at once".[21] Hence, in his stage and filmed productions of *Trilby*, he incorporated elements of burlesque with restrained and rhetorical acting codes, and drew on his stage personality to move between the codes.

However, this interchangeability created contradictory critical responses. While some critics felt that there was no acting ability to comment on, others were less disparaging and acknowledged the pictorial qualities of Tree's performance. For example, Tree's interpretation of Svengali was noted for its "picturesque" acting by the critic of *The Manchester Guardian* (9 September 1895). By November, Tree had made some alterations to his part, enough to bring the character into "greater or less prominence". The critic of *The Era* in November 1895 commented favourably on the presentational codes of his melodramatic performance:

> The slight sketches of subordinate character are necessarily moved into the background, and *Svengali* is made to loom up tremendously, Satanically. And wonderfully does Mr Beerbohm Tree depict the overpowering Jew. His make-up is a study in itself. This *Svengali* towers above his companions with the pride of Lucifer and the malice of Mephistopheles. In the first act his very old clothes are suggestive and poetic. And how weird are the bursts of this *Svengali's* merriment.[22]

Svengali's merriment was also distinguished by a use of farce, which was disliked by some critics who complained about the more popular, burlesque use of red noses for the Laird and the tipsy soldiers, and the use of the cancan.[23]

The use of comedy in the stage production is also transcribed to the screen version. Indeed, film comedy also draws on presentational codes of performance in films of this period with characters playing to the front of the screen and acknowledging their audiences by direct address to the camera. In *Trilby*, Svengali assumes most of the humour with his mockery of the student artists' conservative status – blowing smoke at them is just one example. His comic actions also include the insolent kick of his leg, which had caused so much enjoyment for audiences in the stage version. This use of the burlesque also echoes the variety format of the music-hall with its mixed programming, and here we see Tree's attempts to appeal to all classes of his audience in the film version.

To conclude, the film version of *Trilby* incorporated the same tension between the different performance practices as had been evident in the stage play. Tree uses comic effects to relieve dramatic intensity while effectively using presentational codes to heighten the magnitude, grotesqueness and diabolic character of Svengali. And while critics may have been developing a taste for a more restrained style in acting codes, the melodramatic conventions still retained their popular appeal well into the 20th century.

Notes

[1]   Available as part of the *British Silent Film Compilation* on British Film Institute Online.

[2]   Rachael Low, *The History of the British Film 1906-1914* (London: George Allen & Unwin, 1949): 129-130.

[3]   Ibid: 119.

[4]   Publicity brochure for *Henry VIII*, February 1911, quoted in ibid: 186-187.

[5]   "The Picture Theatre, Trilby Filmed" undated cutting from *The Sunday Times*, from a selection of press cuttings in the Herbert Beerbohm Tree's press cuttings book, held in the Herbert Beerbohm Tree Collection. This collection is housed at the University of Bristol. However, I have used the microfiche edition (Unplaced; Emmett Publishing, 1989) of the Collection at the Shakespeare Centre Library in Stratford on Avon. All following citations will be relevant to this edition.

[6]   Low: 111.

[7]   *The Bioscope* 9 April 1914: 172, quoted in ibid: 258.

[8]   *Trilby* (1914), directed by Harold Shaw, one-reel viewing copy held at the National Film and Television Archive (NFTVA), London.

[9]   See "'Trilby': London Film Company's Fine Production", *The Bioscope* 24: 404 (9 July 1914): 130-131, for comments on the trade show of *Trilby*, held on 2 July 1914 at the West End Theatre, London, and for a discussion of the whole film.

[10]   However, *The Bioscope* review (ibid: 131) notes that "[t]he sequence of the story is admirably maintained, and the termination of the book, which, with all the charm of Gecko's pathetic narration, provides something of a dramatic anti-climax, has been judiciously condensed"; and "remarkable in their effect" are "the scenes in the studio". Svengali's death is also referred to as giving "pictures which are as impressive as anything the stage can produce".

[11]   Charles Musser, "The Nickelodeon Era Begins: Establishing the Framework for Hollywood's Mode of Representation", in Thomas Elsaesser with Adam Barker (eds), *Early Cinema: Space Frame Narrative* (London: British Film Institute, 1990): 268.

[12]   As found in the Herbert Beerbohm Tree Collection. No authorship is attributed to the cinema plot.

[13]   A Nicholas Vardac, *Stage to Screen: Theatrical Method from Garrick to Griffith* (Cambridge: Havard University Press, 1949): xvii-xviii.

[14]   Paul Potter, "*Trilby* (1914)", in George Taylor (ed), *Trilby* (Oxford; New York: Oxford University Press, 1996): 219.

[15]   The following stage prompts refer to the lighting changes.

[16]   "'Trilby': London Film Company's Fine Production": 131.

[17]   Janet Staiger, "The Eyes Are Really the Focus: Photoplay Acting and Film Form and Style", *Wide Angle* 6: 4 (1984): 15.

[18]   See Christine Gledhill (ed), *Home Is Where the Heart Is: Studies in Melodrama and*

the Woman's Film (London: British Film Institute, 1987): 26.

[19]   In the Herbert Beerbohm Tree Collection.

[20]   Ibid.

[21]   W L Courtney, "An Open Letter to an American Friend", in *Herbert Beerbohm Tree: Some Memories of Him and of His Art Collected by Max Beerbohm*, second edition (London: Hutchinson & Co., n.d.): 264.

[22]   Quoted in *The Golden Age of Melodrama: Twelve 19th Century Melodramas*, abridged and introduced by Michael Kilgarriff (London: Wolfe Publishing, 1974): 474. Emphasis in original.

[23]   *The Illustrated London News* 107 (21) (September 1895).

Fred Karno's Music-Hall, Copyright and Silent Film Comedy

Frank Scheide

Fred Karno's music-hall, 1895-1908

"Fred Karno didn't teach Charlie [Chaplin] and me all we know about comedy", Stan Laurel once told his biographer, John McCabe. "He just taught us most of it".[1] Few impresarios had greater success in the English music-hall than Fred Karno (1866-1941), whose work greatly influenced the early history of the motion picture. A number of Karno sketches and a substantial amount of his comic business were converted from stage to screen by former employees such as Chaplin and Laurel. Karno also initiated one of the first lawsuits involving film and copyright infringement in British jurisprudence.

Frederick John Westcott was born into a working-class family in Exeter in 1866, but spent most of his early life in Nottingham, after the family moved there in 1875. Apprenticed to a plumber while still a teenager, Fred became interested in a show-business career after performing gymnastics on-stage in an amateur competition at the Nottingham Alhambra Theatre. He gave up plumbing as a vocation at the age of eighteen, and formed a music-hall act with a wire-walker and juggler. In 1887, the 21-year-old performer ended up at "Poverty Corner" near London's Waterloo Bridge – a location where music-hall entertainers congregated while looking for work. When a group called The Three Carnos failed to appear for a vaudeville engagement, Fred and two other unemployed gymnasts agreed to impersonate the act. The substitute trio was so successful that they were given a month's work using their predecessors' name. To prevent them from being confused with the original artistes, the new act changed the "C" in Carno to a "K", and Fred's stage cognomen was born.[2]

The foundation of Karno's art and earliest show-business training centred around gymnastic routines that were improvised and choreographed in practice, rather than translated from a written script. These intricately synchronised movements, involving several athletes, were presented without dialogue and incorporated split-second timing. Karno's ability to perform as a speechless comedian enabled him to make the transition from acrobat to actor in a number of silent circus skits early in his career. *Love in a Tub*, the first successful music-hall comedy sketch in which Karno appeared, was done entirely in mime.

The British tradition of performing sketches in mime goes back at least to the 18th century when "patent theatres" were able to ban theatrical dialogue from performances in unauthorised establishments. A "patent" was the preferential approval, granted by the government, that gave a theatre the right to stage theatrical entertainments. This patent requirement enabled the government both to control the number of theatres in England, and to censor the content of their plays. Venues that staged alternative forms of entertainment – such as singing, dancing or acrobatics – did not need a patent. However, these establishments were subject to prosecution if they performed anything deemed to be within the province of the patent theatres. (A clown named Delpini was actually sent to prison in 1701 for saying the words "roast beef" without authorisation during a Christmas performance in a non-patent theatre.) By 1901, the silent sketch had long been popular as a turn in English variety, and Karno was one of the industry's most successful producers of short comic narratives.[3]

Karno wrote and produced the first of his own sketches, *Hilarity*, in January 1895. More revue than story, *Hilarity* was an instant success, and toured for the next five years. Part of the comic incongruity of these skits was achieved by placing "red-nosed" clowns in the midst of what otherwise were fairly realistic-looking people and settings. Comedians such as Chaplin, Stan Laurel, Billie Reeves, Billie Ritchie and Fred "Pimple" Evans became variety stars wearing the exaggerated make-up and baggy trousers of the music-hall eccentric. These same artistes later adapted variations of their stage characterisations and Karno routines for their film comedies.

Finding sketch production more profitable and less physically demanding than being an acrobat, Karno gave up performing before the end of the 19th century. One of his earliest successes, *Jail Birds*, was produced just prior to 1900. The skit was based on stories about incompetent burglars that Karno heard from prison inmates while working in a jail as a plumber's assistant. According to a 1904 review of *Jail Birds* in the entertainment trade journal *The Era*, "three noisy burglars enter [an] apartment by the window and apparently take every means in their power to make their presence known to the sleeping occupants of the house".[4] Chaplin used a similar situation involving noisy housebreakers in his 1916 Essanay comedy, *Police*. Karno later reworked *Jail Birds* into two other skits, *His Majesty's Guests* (1902) and *Dandy Thieves* (1906). The theme of incompetent individuals attempting to get into a house was also the basis for another successful Karno sketch, *The Bailiffs*, produced in 1907.

Described as "a tale of slum-land...with a distinct note of drama", *Early Birds* was one of Karno's favourite sketches. First performed in 1901, the pantomime in *Early Birds* was accompanied by "beautiful incidental music". The production also utilised elaborate machinery that enabled a slum scene to be transformed into a handsomely furnished interior. "Birds" was used in the title so that the sketch could be associated with Karno's previous stage success, *Jail Birds*. Although Karno's name was becoming synonymous with low comedy, this showman wanted to be known for more than slapstick at this time. By combining comedy with drama, and contrasting slum life with the world of the middle class in *Early Birds*, Karno sought to broaden his narrative expression and audience appeal. Chaplin would have the same concerns when he later made film comedies such as *The Vagabond* (1916) and *The Kid* (1921).

Karno desired to gain respectability from his music-hall material at the turn of the century, but his association with slapstick would forever limit what he could do on the stage. His attempt to produce a dramatic American play entitled *Marked for Life* in 1902 failed because audiences were expecting something funny. Despite its commercial failure, *Marked for Life* convinced the music-hall producer that it was time that he experimented with dialogue in his next comic sketch, *His Majesty's Guests*. A biography of Karno justified his illegal use of theatrical speech with the statement, "Some laws are certainly made to be broken". *His Majesty's Guests*, a "talking version" of *Jail Birds*, proved very popular. Its success enabled the leading actor Fred Kitchen, in his first Karno collaboration, to become a music-hall star.[5]

Chaplin joined Karno in 1908, and was a featured player until he left the company to make films for Mack Sennett in 1913. Despite the introduction of dialogue, choreography continued to be a very important component of the Karno sketch. According to Chaplin:

> At the time [I joined Karno] he had between eighteen and twenty companies touring all over England and in many parts of the world, America, South America and Africa. No language was necessary because the acting of the troupe was vivid and expressive enough to bring laughter from any race. All of the pieces we did, as I remember them, were cruel and boisterous, filled with acrobatic humor and low, knockabout comedy. Each man working for Karno had to have perfect timing and had to know the peculiarities of everyone else in the cast so that we could, collectively, achieve a cast tempo.
>
> It took about a year for an actor to get the repertoire of a dozen shows down pat. Karno required us to know a number of parts so that the players could be interchanged. When one left the company it was like taking a screw or a pin out of a very delicate piece of machinery.[6]

It is interesting to note that, when making his film comedies, Chaplin surrounded himself with a stock company of actors who could adapt to his working methods.

As film historians Kevin Brownlow and David Gill made evident in their 1982 documentary series *The Unknown Chaplin*, Chaplin did not work with a film script. Rather, he would start with a premise and improvise before the camera until he isolated the particular comic business he wanted to do. Once he knew what he was doing, Chaplin would shoot scenes repeatedly until the acting and tempo of each segment satisfied his demanding expectations.

One of Karno's most lucrative formulas was to develop sketches that parodied popular entertainments. *The Yap Yaps* (1906) centred around boxing, and the focus of *The Football Match* (1906) is apparent from its title. By far the most successful of these Karno parodies was *Mumming Birds* (1904), which made fun of the music-hall itself.

Fred Karno's *Mumming Birds* and music-hall self-reflexivity

In the theatre, the focus of the performance is usually on a play performed by actors who behave as if the audience is not there. The setting depicted on-stage is treated as if it is totally separate from the world and a space in which the spectators are sitting. In contrast, the music-hall entertainer generally acknowledges the spectator during a performance, and even exchanges comments with individual audience-members. The tendency of music-hall turns to remind audiences that they were experiencing music-hall as they watched it gave this entertainment a more self-referential focus than that found in theatre. *Mumming Birds* was particularly self-reflexive in that it was a music-hall sketch that parodied the music-hall experience.[7]

Karno actually got the idea for *Mumming Birds* from a show called *Entertaining the Shah*, put on by a music-hall fraternity called "The Grand Order of Water Rats" in honour of the Shah of Persia when he was in England in 1904. While not caring much for this particular burlesque of a typical music-hall programme, Karno saw possibilities in the concept. The new title of *Mumming Birds* was chosen because of its association with Karno's two earlier "bird" productions. In the United States the skit was called *A Night in an English Music Hall*. When *Remember Fred Karno?* was published in 1939, the producer's biographers claimed that *Mumming Birds* was still being performed, 35 years after its debut.[8]

One of the earliest reviews of *Mumming Birds* can be found in *The Era* in June 1904, written when the sketch was appearing at the Canterbury Music Hall on Westminster Bridge Road:

> The programme that is arranged under the direction of Mr George Adney Payne at the palace over the water is nightly sampled by a mirth-loving crowd of South Londoners, who positively shout with laughter at the new production by Mr Fred Karno's comedians entitled *Mumming Birds*, which has been seen at other London halls under the differing titles of *Twice Nightly* and *A Stage Within a Stage*. The fun arises mostly from the behaviour of certain occupants of the boxes of a temporary theatre fixed up on the stage, where a variety entertainment is in progress. The extempore and topical singer persists in composing verses about the wrong people, and is pelted by a terrible boy in the o.p. box; a ballad singer, most amusingly indistinct, evidently possesses fascinations for the funny individual in the prompt-side box, who is in a happy state of intoxication. Then there is the short-skirted damsel who deprecates in song and dance the doings of the naughty, naughty men; and the fun is on the up grade during the tricks of the conjuror. It, however, becomes uproarious with the announcement of the great Marconi, the 'terrible Turkey,' who is prepared to wrestle all comers, and who will forfeit twenty-five pounds if he fail to 'pin' any opponent in five seconds. The challenge is immediately taken up by one of the troupe seated among the audience. But the laughter is loudest when the inebriated one before referred to, who has shown his dissatisfaction with the show in various ways, prepares himself for a contest with the wrestler, and eventually, after some droll falling about business, 'downs' him, claiming the promised reward of £25. A general melée ensues, and the curtains close in on an uproarious scene. The chief factors in the drollery are the gentleman with 'the vine leaves in his hair,' as Ibsen puts it, and the big boy. A finer exhibition of the dazed condition due to an advanced stage of drunkenness we have not seen on the variety stage, and it would be difficult to overpraise such really clever work. To the smaller comedian who plays the boy much credit must be given for his smartness in promoting the hilarity that becomes general during the progress of the sketch, which should certainly sustain, if not enhance, the reputation of the celebrated troupe playing it.[9]

As can be seen from this review, *Mumming Birds* was both a reflection and a parody of the self-reflexive nature of the music-hall. Some of the Karno actors played disgruntled music-hall spectators who berated the performances of other Karno players pretending to be horrible variety artistes. The acts themselves could be parodies of recognisable performances that patrons were currently seeing in the halls.

In January 1904, *The Era* noted that the country was currently enjoying a "wrestling boom". The "Terrible Turkey" of *Mumming Birds* may have been referring to an "Ahmed Madrali", who billed himself as the "'Terrible Turk'...the undefeated champion of the world". Jimmy Aubrey, a former Karno performer who made film comedies with Stan Laurel for producer Joe Rock in America, may have originated the role of the "'Terrible Turkey". Aubrey demonstrated how he posed as the character for film historian Sam Gill during an interview in Los Angeles many years later. *The Era* singled out comedian Billie Reeves by name for his role of the comic drunk a year later.[10]

Karno's self-reflexive staging of this entertainment that burlesqued itself was so successful that others began imitating him. Unauthorised versions of *Mumming Birds* were appearing in Germany and the United States by 1906. Many of the American "bootleg" editions featured former Karno players. In a 1907 advertisement in *The Era*, Karno was to state: "Members of the Profession will perhaps be pleased to know that I have succeeded in my action in the American Courts for Pirating my Sketch, '*Mumming Birds*'. Intending Pirates will please note that I intend to take the most stringent action against the offenders in this respect." Although he enjoyed some successful litigation in stopping the piracy of *Mumming Birds* on-stage, this sketch was to be adapted for film in ways that Karno would never reverse in court.[11]

Karno v. Pathé Frères (Limited) and the decline of Karno's music-hall

In the 2 February 1907 issue of *The Era*, Pathé Frères of London advertised a film entitled *At the Music Hall* among its latest releases. The film was described as "[a] variety of turns and scenes at an up-to-date Music Hall, showing tumblers, singers, dancers and conjurers. Very amusing, and a great draw just now." The film featured an unbilled Max Linder. Karno challenged Pathé in court, claiming that the company had produced an unauthorised motion picture based on his music-hall sketch *Mumming Birds*. It was one of the first cases involving motion pictures and copyright infringement in England.[12]

Extensive excerpts from the court proceedings of "Karno v. Pathé Frères (Limited)" were printed in both *The Era* and *The Times* as the trial progressed. Judgment was eventually made in favour of the defendants. While recognising that the film was definitely patterned after the stage production known as *Mumming Birds*, the court believed that it was the exhibitor, if anyone, who should be held responsible for copyright violation. This ruling established a precedent that it was legal to manufacture a plagiarised film, but the exhibitor might be breaking the law in showing it. Karno later joked that the court said he should have sued the projectionist.[13]

A dubious judgment, the case of "Karno v. Pathé Frères (Limited)" reflected the continued problem of defining variety entertainment within current law. To speak on-stage was technically illegal, if one was not performing in a "legitimate theatre", but to perform in mime meant trying to protect one's material using copyright laws developed around the written word. Since the content of Karno's skits varied from performance to performance, identifying a sketch for copyright purposes could be difficult. One method was to print a relatively detailed description of the plot in trade journals such as *The Era* for "copyright purposes". The first Karno skit listed in this fashion appears to have been *The Old Master*, which was described in *The Era* on 2 March 1907. The practice of filing plot descriptions, together with the ruling from another court case entitled "Tate v. Fullbrook", seems to have settled some of the problems of unauthorised performances, at least on-stage. In the case of Tate v. Fullbrook, the comedian Harry Tate claimed that his popular sketch *Motoring* had been performed by the defendant. Duplication of dialogue, gags, number of characters and set design from

Motoring in the unauthorised production supported Tate's claim. The case established a precedent for the recognition of copyright of non-verbal or comic business in a sketch when taken as a whole. The ruling did not necessarily protect every element of a work, such as individual jokes. While this judgment allowed someone to steal a "gag", it made it more difficult to "lift" an entire act. Unfortunately for Karno, these precedents were ignored when applied to an unauthorised version of *Mumming Birds* presented on film.[14]

Given Karno's failed lawsuit, it is probably not surprising that Chaplin would later make his own film version of *Mumming Birds* for Essanay, *A Night in the Show*, in 1915. Since there had been a 1907 film based on this subject, Chaplin's *A Night in the Show* might also be called a "remake". In 1929, the English comedian Lupino Lane appeared in a short Hollywood film, *Only Me*, for Educational Pictures. The form and content of *Only Me* appear to have been even closer to Karno's *Mumming Birds* than Chaplin's picture, and contained the added attraction of Lane playing all twenty-plus characters!

Karno was to lose more than the film rights to *Mumming Birds*. During the First World War, the motion picture, and Chaplin's films in particular, stole audiences away from the music-hall. English variety continued to exist after 1918, but the music-hall would never enjoy the popularity it had known prior to the Great War. It must have seemed to Karno that everyone could profit from putting his comedy on film with the exception of himself. Karno's name was associated with filmmaking in the 1920s and 1930s, but to little success. He died in 1941, leaving an estate of £42 7s 4d. Ironically, the very films that probably most irritated the music-hall producer may contain the best record of Fred Karno's comedy available to us today.[15]

Notes

[1]   John McCabe, *Charlie Chaplin* (London: Robson Books, 1978): 27. Much of the research used in this study was originally carried out for my doctoral dissertation, *The History of Low Comedy and 19th and Early 20th Century English Music Hall as a Basis for Examining the 1914-1917 Films of Charles Spencer Chaplin*, a thesis submitted in partial fulfilment of requirements for the degree of Doctor of Philosophy (Communication Arts) at the University of Wisconsin-Madison, 1990. A review I wrote on the history of Karno's *Mumming Birds* and "Karno v. Pathé Frères (Limited)" were published under the title "His Prehistoric Past" in *Limelight* 4: 1 (1998): 3.

[2]   The best biographies on Karno are Edwin Adeler and Con West, *Remember Fred Karno?: The Life of a Great Showman* (London: John Long, 1939), and J P Gallagher, *Fred Karno: Master of Mirth and Tears* (London: Robert Hale & Company, 1971).

[3]   Frank Scheide, "Legitimate Theater vs. The English Music Hall: The Legal Repression of Dramatic Expression on London's Variety Stage, 1899-1912", *Free Speech Yearbook* 28 (1990): 120-131.

[4]   "The London Music Halls: South London", *The Era* 67: 3408 (16 January 1904): 23.

[5]   Gallagher: 46-56, 76-77; Adeler and West: 89-93, 99-100.

[6]   Quoted in McCabe: 28-29.

[7]   Frank Scheide, "The influence of the English music-hall on early screen acting", in Linda Fitzsimmons and Sarah Street (eds), *Moving Performance: British Stage and Screen, 1890s-1920s* (Trowbridge: Flicks Books, 2000): 71.

[8]   Adeler and West: 118-124.

[9]   "The London Music Halls: The Canterbury", *The Era* 67: 3430 (18 June 1904): 19.

[10]   "The London Music Halls: The London Pavilion", *The Era* 67: 3408 (16 January 1904): 23; conversation between the author and Sam Gill, archivist emeritus, the Academy

of Motion Picture Arts and Sciences, 20 May 1999; and *The Era* 29 July 1905: 19.

[11]   *The Era* 5 January 1907: 27; Adeler and West: 122-124.

[12]   Pathé Frères, London, advertisement, *The Era* 2 February 1907: 34.

[13]   "Karno v. Pathé Frères (Limited). Alleged Infringement of Copyright by Cinematograph", *The Times* 4 April 1908: 4; "Karno v. Pathé Frères (Limited). Alleged Infringement of Copyright by Cinematograph", *The Times* 7 April 1908: 4; "A Question of Copyright", *The Era* 11 April 1908: 21; "Karno v. Pathé Frères (London). Alleged Infringement of Copyright by Cinematograph", *The Times* 30 April 1908: 3; and "Copyright v. Camera Right. Important Judgment", *The Era* 71: 3632 (2 May 1908): 24-25.

[14]   "Copyright v. Camera Right. Important Judgment": 24-25.

[15]   I am grateful to Tony Fletcher for pointing out that film versions of *Mumming Birds* and *Early Birds* were made in England in 1922/23. While Karno was given credit for scenario in the credits, it is not clear how involved he was with their production and the films no longer seem to exist. Fred Karno would go bankrupt in 1926. The National Film and Television Archive (NFTVA) has a viewing copy of Karno's 1932 talkie *The Bailiffs* with Flanagan and Allen, which features Fred in a delightful cameo. Gallagher (167) lists the assets of Karno's estate.

"Cultivating Pimple": Performance Traditions and the Film Comedy of Fred and Joe Evans

Michael Hammond

On 3 July 1915, an article entitled "Britain's Greatest Film Players" appeared in the fan magazine *Pictures and the Picturegoer*. The article published the results of a poll which listed six picture personalities as their readers' favourites. In descending order, the six were: Alma Taylor, Elisabeth Risden, Charles Chaplin, Stewart Rome, Chrissie White and Fred Evans. Apart from Chaplin, all were personalities within the British film industry. The last figure, Fred Evans, was better-known as "Pimple", and such was his popularity that he could be referred to as the picture personality "you *all* know".[1] The fact that only two of the six winners were comedians, and that the summer of 1915 was in fact "Chaplin's summer" in both Britain and the United States, is a testament to the level of popularity enjoyed by Pimple.

Film historians and critics have only half-recognised Pimple's popularity as a significant feature of the middle silent period of British cinema, but all too often have simply reproduced the dismissive tones reserved for British cinema generally and for British comedy cinema in particular. Rachael Low describes Pimple within a broader assessment of British comedy films which unfailingly fall below the standard set by American comedy films. Characterising the end of the war as some kind of watershed where British comedy had emerged from the "lower class domestic circle" to a stage where "unselfconscious mirth at physical discomfort or humiliation was now concealed and subjects of greater subtlety were necessary as vehicles for such cruel jokes", Low places Pimple below British comedians such as Billy Merson, George Robey and Lupino Lane – a hierarchy that had itself been distinctly overshadowed by Charlie Chaplin and also most American comedy generally.[2] This eclipse by American comedy films in terms of performance and story was believed to be matched by a corresponding lack of advancement of filmic technique. It is revealing that, in Low's account, Pimple receives the most attention in the opening paragraph of the section on cartoon films. *Pimple Enlists* (1914) is cited as one of the few live comedy films in which the war was the object of ridicule, since, for Pimple, "few things were sacred".[3]

A less dismissive view of Pimple is provided by John Montgomery, who recognises Fred Evans' work as burlesquing life as well as current stage and film successes, and is more than "simple knockabout comedy". Yet again, while providing an account of some of the significant developments in early comedy cinema in Britain, this assessment is predicated on a comparison with the American film: "Could some of the youngsters have done better in America, where during the 1914 war the movie industry expanded while the British film business slumped?".[4] He notes three examples of those who had: Chaplin, Stan Laurel and the limited success of Lupino Lane.

In contrast, Andy Medhurst recognises the tendency to foreground Hollywood in most histories of film comedy, and notes that "it should not be forgotten how many of these [Hollywood exponents] had learned their trade in the British halls".[5] He argues that, while comedians such as Pimple are "less than central to film histories with commitments to privileging stylistic forms or directorial authorship", they are evidence of a need to recognise the role that British music-hall played in defining the social function of the cinema.[6] Writing over 30 years after Low and Montgomery, Medhurst provides the first instance of considering British comedy, and to some extent Pimple, in a manner which neither compares the British comedy film unfavourably with Hollywood, nor sees the period as a "lost opportunity" for British cinema in general.

In all these accounts, Pimple sits as emblematic of the fate and function of British comedy in the 1910s, at the moment when Hollywood began truly to dominate British screens. This essay seeks to suggest that a consideration of the performance traditions of music-hall provides a depth of perspective about the place of Pimple as a picture personality and Fred Evans as a comedy filmmaker within the cinema culture of Britain in the period 1912-18.

Pimple's popularity is significant throughout these years. Even a cursory glance at the trade papers and fan magazines of the period reveals a considerable presence of Pimple films and articles, either by him or about him. His output of films is considerable even by the standard of the day, with the production of a film a week at the height of his powers in the period 1914-17. Based on this presence in the trade and fan journals, his mention in local press advertisements, and an output sustained over a lengthy period, it is safe to assume that his popularity with audiences was on a level with the pre-Chaplin Keystones and the Max Linder Pathé comedies. The Pimple films are instructive in terms of the place of British comedy films of the period in national film culture: not only by what they reveal in terms of the ways in which audiences made sense of them, particularly the role of audience familiarity with the Pimple "burlesques", but also because they allow a deeper perspective on the constituency of British film audiences during the war, a time of significant demographic upheaval. Moreover, Evans is popular at a moment in film history which sees the rise of the classical Hollywood style and mode of production, and the move from the open market to the system of exclusives, in which distribution networks became more centralised and production companies began to deal directly with exhibitors, ultimately leading to a system which favoured the Hollywood companies. It is evident throughout that Evans acknowledged these shifts, working with the burlesque form but incorporating strategies which built his image as a star personality beyond the screen.

In an interview with Denis Gifford in 1966, Joe Evans talked at length about his work with his brother Fred. He gives an account of Fred Evans' career from his work at Cricks and Martin in the "Charlie Smiler" films:

> He [Evans] told them he was a good knockabout and acrobat, and they gave him a small part. They were so pleased with his work that they gave him a bigger part, and a bigger part, until finally they decided to run a series around him. He went under the name of Charlie Smiler...He had a strange make-up on, no red nose or anything, Max Linder style: a silk hat, frock coat, fancy waistcoat, spats, a little moustache and a walking stick. He did a very successful series – 'Charlie Smiler Does This', 'Charlie Smiler Does That', 'Rides a Bike', 'Goes Courting', and so on – finishing up with the usual chase of course. They were very hot on chases, rushing through the street, knocking everybody over![7]

In Evans' own account, he met Cricks and Martin at his Uncle Will Evans' house. Will had had success in a number of screen adaptations of his music-hall sketches such as *Whitewashing the Ceiling* (1912), a knockabout in which he appeared with Arthur Conquest. In the interview, Fred says that he was asked by Cricks and Martin at that first meeting to play Charlie Smiler, which he referred to as "a 'dude' series": "I made a funny fall, which so pleased them (and didn't hurt me) that they asked me if I could write a film plot. I wrote and played in 'Prescribed by the Doctor,' and got £5 for it."[8] According to his brother Joe, he joined Fred while he was doing Charlie Smiler, "playing little parts, playing 'as cast'".[9] After leaving Cricks and Martin over a dispute about money, Fred began working for a film company called Precision run by a cinema exhibitor, Radcliffe, who had a studio at Whipp's Cross. Joe had been putting on melodramas in Dover, but he quit to help his brother Fred write scripts because those that Radcliffe had been giving him were "utterly useless".

After a short stay, they left Radcliffe, who had interpreted their contracts to include ushering at his cinema, to form their own film company, with finance from relatives and friends based in the music-hall. Working within the already existing tradition of the music-hall sketch with a comic personality, the two brothers began to develop a character within the "dude" genre. Although described as a Max Linder type, this character, recognisable by music-hall and cinema audiences alike, employed a use of make-up that was peculiar to British music-hall comedy. Mack Sennett gives an adequate description of this type of make-up in his account of the night he and Mabel Normand first saw Chaplin in Fred Karno's *A Night in an English Music Hall* (renamed for the United States from its original *Mumming Birds* [1904]):

> We caught one act...which was more hilarious than anything at Hammerstein's. A 'little Englisher,' as Mabel called him, duded up in a frock coat, played the part of a drunken spectator in a box. He seemed about forty-five years old. He got into the act on stage, of course, and took part in a knockabout comic fight with the other English actors. The most striking effect of his make-up was an enormous red nose.
> 'Feller's pretty funny,' Mabel said.
> 'Think he'd be good for pictures?' I said.
> 'He might be,' Mabel said. 'Isn't this the man you were asking Hank Mann about?'...
> 'I don't know,' I said to Mabel. 'He has all the tricks and routines and he can take a fall, and probably do a 108, but that limey make-up and costume – I don't know.'[10]

Sennett's misgivings about the "enormous red nose" and the "limey make-up" are no doubt based on what he knew would work on film, and highlight the English music-hall and pantomime traditions as alien to US cinema audiences. By contrast, Evans' use of make-up in this tradition was indispensable to the creation of Pimple. The Pimple character was developed under the auspices of the new film company Ec-Ko. There are a number of stories about how the name originated. Montgomery records that Pimple was "a clown-faced comedian with curly hair, and it is said that when he first appeared on the screen wearing a little cap perched on top of his head, the children all shouted out 'Pimple!' and so gave him his name".[11] Two more plausible stories come from the brothers. According to Fred, Pimple was the name of a clown he had played when he was with Sanger's Circus. Joe's story is that Fred thought it up while in response to Cricks and Martin's threat to sue if they used the Charlie Smiler character.

Joe's story is the most plausible in that he recounts that they were indeed working on a "dude"-type character along the lines of Charlie Smiler when Cricks and Martin issued their threat to sue. In response, they not only changed the name of the character, but also very likely the name followed their decision to change from the "dude" persona to a more clownlike character. In an interesting reversal of Chaplin's move from "limey make-up", the Evans brothers moved towards it. Taking on the characteristics of the circus clown, the Pimple make-up was distinct, and is consistent in all the films which still exist. There are two photographs from April 1915: one which shows Fred Evans in a white tie and black jacket, the show business gentleman; and a second as Pimple. As both the films and the photographs are in black and white, it is difficult to tell whether the whole of the face is painted. It appears to be white make-up covering the nose and mouth area from just above the tip of the nose along the creases in the face, which extend to the corners of the mouth and then from the corners to the tip of the chin. There are heavy lines which outline the white make-up, and there are two lines drawn from the nostrils to give the impression of an upturned nose. It is apparent from his films that the teeth are blackened to give the impression of the foolish grin of a circus clown.

Pimple's costume is remembered by Joe as consisting of "a little cricket cap on his head, long hair down the sides of his face, parted in the centre, and a bricket [cricket] blazer. I always remember the green and yellow stripes, muffler round his neck, big baggy trousers and big boots."[12] Unlike Chaplin's tramp, which Charles Musser has suggested was based on the actual dress of tramps in the US, this make-up and costume drew particularly on the traditions of clowns and pantomime.[13] It is important here to pay closer attention to the way this make-up and costume operate in the Pimple films. The meaning of "Pimple" suggests a distortion of order, and has a link with the "red nose" tradition of clown make-up. A contemporary reference to Pimple's name by a fan, one Lydia Shroebree of Northfleet, gives testament to the humorous connotations of the name. After stating her wish that he would visit their little cinema, she states: "We are going to organise a Pimple Club of lady members, all of whom must cultivate pimples, the most conspicuous to take the lead. Now how do you think that will go?". She goes on to make specific reference to his nose: "I have a weakness for turned up noses (red ones in particular) and yours, sweetheart, is about the rosiest nosey I have ever seen. It has such a cute little tilt; in fact, it is all tilt."[14] No doubt tongue-in-cheek, the letter emphasises interaction with Pimple's persona in the same way that imitations of Chaplin's walk, his "cute" little moustache and the lookalike contests that were ubiquitous from 1915-17 in Britain were a means by which fans engaged with the comic personality – an expression of familiarity which was a staple in the audience engagement with comic stars in music-hall.

The antecedents of the make-up and the costume lay in the harlequinade clown. The make-up is the distinguishing feature, and marks Pimple out as the main instigator of chaos and mirth. Lois Rutherford has called attention to a number of historians who have traced the origins of the music-hall sketch artist to the harlequinade and the pantomime clown, particularly the influence of Grimaldi's "Joey", and to the theatrical farce genre in legitimate theatre.[15] This "Lord of Misrule" characteristic is evident in a number of Pimple films of the "chase" type. Pimple's *Motor Bike* (1913) has as its setting an "everyday life" street scene. Pimple notices a motor bike for sale, and later finds a wallet and buys the machine. In the character of the gentleman clown, he tips the salesman who delivers the bike, and then rides through the city creating destruction. The characters he annoys are significant ones. Firstly, he almost hits a policeman, then runs over a bricklayer. Next he hits a suffragette (a male actor, probably his brother Joe, in drag) who is giving a speech from a podium to an all-male audience, and who reacts by taking a plank from the podium and beats him. He then hits a gardener and a fence painter, both of whom beat him. He then hits a brick wall which collapses on people having a picnic, and they throw bricks at him. He rides into a punting boat with two men and a woman in it, and the film ends with him demolishing a four-wheeled carriage and horses. The combination of clown and modern machine disrupts regardless of class boundaries, but it holds particularly extended gags for the suffragette, the punters and the upper-class carriage. Pimple, like the Chaplin tramp, disrupts the work space and the temporal and spatial boundaries which contain or occupy the workmen such as the bricklayer, the fence painter or the gardener. The serendipity of finding the wallet ensures his ability to transgress and transcend social boundaries. The suffragette must be seen here as a folk devil representing the kind of social respectability associated with temperance reformers, and a common target of abuse throughout music-hall and the earliest comic films.

The earlier Pimple chase films draw upon the rudiments of the music-hall sketch by incorporating recognisable character types, but the chase films were not particularly distinguishable from other comedy films shown from 1912 to early 1914. Joe Evans records that they worked on developing the Pimple persona along the lines of the comic sketch "series": "We did Pimple as a policeman, Pimple as a postman, a sailor, this and that until I finally ran out of ideas".[16] The turn to burlesque in the Pimple films stands out in Joe Evans' mind as significant to developing the character beyond chase and knockabout. Inspired by the release of British and Colonial's (B&C's) *The Battle of Waterloo* (1913), Evans wrote a script focusing on verbal, as well as physical, spoof:

> I went home and wrote it. I gave him Napoleon's hat with his famous quiff stuck on the brim, so when he took it off it came with it!...B&C had put in the supposedly true scene where Napoleon comes to a sentry and does sentry duty for him. So I had Pimple come on, pick up the gun, and the sentry wakes up, grabs it, bashes Napoleon over the head with it and says, 'No you don't, I've missed things like that before!'[17]

The move to burlesquing theatrical productions, big-budget films and current issues was important for the Evans brothers, as it shows their response to both the popularity of Pimple and the consistent demand for new product which the open-market system of film distribution created. From the outset, this system had created a demand for films which rivalled that of the United States. Kristin Thompson has demonstrated that, while the market for films in the United States was larger, the shelf life of a film in Britain at this time was much shorter. This was largely due to the difference in geographical distribution of audiences. In the United States, it could take between six months and a year for a film to reach a majority percentage of theatres, whereas in Britain, where the cities were much closer and populations denser, a film could reach market saturation within 90 days.[18] By 1914, the trend towards the exclusive feature was significant. By turning towards the "burlesque", the Evans brothers were able simultaneously to produce longer films of topical subjects, with built-in product differentiation and a recognisable personality performing in a format, the comic sketch, with which audiences were already familiar.

By drawing on the "comic sketch form", the Pimple burlesques were also in line with the industry's desire to produce "respectable entertainment". Lois Rutherford suggests that, due to the increasing regulation of music-hall entertainment at the turn of the century, the comic sketch was a desirable halfway point between the comic song and the legitimate theatre. In the case of the comic song, the concern lay mainly in the frequent repetition of the racy refrain, whereas the legitimate theatre was a threat of a different kind: "At the turn of the century, the greatest moral threat was perceived to be lurking in the social and sexual ideas vaunted in the 'new' drama of the legitimate theatre". Compared to both, the sketch was akin to light comedy, and the jokes about, and references to, issues of moral, political or social concern passed by quickly enough to avert any serious attention by moral guardians or official censors. In addition, the sketches "may be regarded as products peculiarly suited to the variety clientele, encompassing both sexes, a range of age groups and social classes, including the educated and 'family' middle-class public".[19]

The Evans brothers were working within the "series" tradition of the comic sketch. In the process of developing the picture personality of Pimple, they were utilising a form which, together with the elementary chase and gag films of the early cinema period, was tailored to the kind of new family audience which the cinema was attracting. The recognisable personality of the comic sketch not only served to secure audiences, as an element of the burgeoning star system, but also provided a form of mediation for potentially distasteful or subversive subjects. Low's comment on *Pimple Enlists* is evidence of that effect, but the Pimple films were talked about in the trade journals and fan magazines in much the same way at the time. *Pictures and the Picturegoer* described *Pimple: Special Constable* (1914) as: "It's all very silly and irresponsible, of course: but then, you know, that is just why 'Pimple' is so funny, and it is good to laugh".[20]

This mediating process, when compared to Chaplin's Keystones and Essanay films, is strikingly explicit. The extant Pimple films often utilise direct address to the camera either in the form of the emblematic shot at the beginning of the film, as a spoof on the introduction of the characters in a serious drama, or more often in the manner of the pantomime aside. In *Pimple Has One* (1915), there is a scene towards the end of the film (which is incomplete) in which Pimple, looking directly at the camera, is sitting with his back to a fence, drunk and exhausted from his exploits. A woman's leg appears in the left of the frame. Pimple, holding a soda bottle, does a double take. The woman's hands appear and begin to unbutton her shoe, which Pimple squirts with soda. She raises her skirt, he pulls it down, she raises it again, he pulls it down. He then reaches for a paint brush and, looking directly at the camera, begins to paint out the left side of the frame, thereby censoring the audience's view as he buttons up her shoe. In this move, the censoring process itself is sent up, but it indicates an interaction with the audience which works to mediate the possible transgression, which, in this case, is enacted by the woman. The scene constructs a consensus between Pimple, the camera and the audience, and allows Pimple a power of controlling the view of the audience/camera, a control which is never misused. This recognition of the Pimple character as having desire is held in check through his consensus with the imagined sensibilities of the audience, a cinema audience anticipated by the established performance traditions of the comic sketch.

In the few extant films, there is a sense of a development of the Pimple character which may not have always been so acquiescent. In *Pimple's Wonderful Gramophone* (1913), Pimple sets up a large box with a protruding megaphone and the words "Wonderful Gramophone – Put a Penny in Slot – Ask For Any Tune You Like & You Will Hear It". Another of the early "everyday life" films, in which characters are disrupted by Pimple's activities, it consists of a parade of recognisable types who try out the machine. Inside is Pimple with an array of musical instruments and noise-makers. The imitation of the imagined perfect modern machine is simultaneously a lampoon on the ineffectivity of automation generally and a spoof on the Gramophone, a relatively new consumer item. At one point in the film, a woman speaks into the megaphone and requests: "I Want Someone to Spoon With Me". Pimple shouts "Bow Wow", comes out of the box, and begins to tickle her. In the style of transgression/punishment of this type of gag, her boyfriend comes into the frame and begins to spank him with a cane. The action of spanking serves to indicate the infantilisation of the Pimple character, a clown who has no sense of proprietorial boundaries. In *Pimple Has One*, the change is distinct. This may be less a chronological development than an indication of the flexibility allowed by the pantomime clown roots of the Pimple character, and, since less than twenty of the 200+ Pimple films are viewable, this can only remain speculative.

The method of burlesque depended, in the comic sketch, on fast dialogue and "verbal slapstick". Pimple "burlesque" films depend to a large extent on the use of intertitles to replace these. Joe Evans' account of the Waterloo sketch shows how they solved this problem through a dependence on the intertitle balanced with sight gags and physical comedy. While, for the modern viewer, this makes these films seem less advanced than the kinetic physical comedy of Sennett's Keystone, Chaplin or Keaton, the source of pleasure in burlesque is audience familiarity with the material being sent up. Popular theatrical productions were a significant part of the Pimple series. In 1914, they made Pimple's *Trilby* following the production by the London Film Company starring Sir Herbert Beerbohm Tree. In this version, Joe Evans played Svengali, and Fred, as Pimple, played Trilby, complete with the grey French soldier's overcoat and the striped short petticoat. This image of Svengali and Trilby was familiar to the popular imagination through pre-existing images that had originated with the drawings that accompanied the serialised version of George Du Maurier's novel in *Harper's Weekly* in 1894, and through the acclaimed stage production of Paul Potter's dramatic adaptation which appeared in the following year at Her Majesty's Theatre. The great popularity of the play and the subsequent parodies, circulating images and critical discussion of the film made the subject ideal for a Pimple burlesque. Sadly, the film itself does not exist, but a photograph of Fred Evans as Pimple in Trilby costume and wig is included in the *Pictures and the Picturegoer* interview. The levels of meaning inherent in the masquerade with Pimple in drag are made even richer by the description of Trilby in the original novel as a "very tall and fully developed young female" who wears a man's slippers which are oversized and cause her feet to drag, and who "would have made a singularly handsome boy".[21] Tangential as this may seem, it does help to explain why Evans chose to have Pimple in the part of Trilby, rather than the villain Svengali. Her clown-like appearance and the unstable nature of her position as a woman and as an object of desire would have allowed Pimple to invoke and to disrupt the erotic visual fascination which is central to both the novel and the film.

The nature of Pimple's burlesques which survive in the National Film and Television Archive (NFTVA), such as *Pimple in The Whip* (1917) and *Pimple's Charge of the Light Brigade* (1914), suggests that the subjects of ridicule and the nature of the comedy are securely within the boundaries of the "socially acceptable". In *Pimple's Charge of the Light Brigade*, the brigade is mustered in what is obviously a leafy English suburb. "The Valley of Death" is a pub into which they all "ride". While recognising the effects of drink, which is a commonly used device in the comedy of this period, there is no real sense in which the jingoistic interpretations of the poem are held up to ridicule. In *Pimple in The Whip*, the play itself is used as a frame to send up, in pantomime fashion, both the topicality of current events and the famous train wreck sequence and the real horse-race on-stage for which the 1909 Drury Lane production by Cecil Raleigh and Henry Hamilton was famous.

The Whip's fame as a play was considerable, and there had been numerous productions since the 1909 version, with extended runs throughout the provinces. The play is about the attempted fixing of a race by two villains, Captain Greville Sartorys and Mrs D'Aquila (Lord Forgivus and Lady Bird in the Pimple version). The villains are depending upon the racehorse "The Whip" losing the race, and, in order to ensure it, Sartorys uncouples the horse car carrying The Whip on the train to Newmarket. The plan is that, a few minutes later, the express train, moving at high speed, will collide with the horse car. The wax museum sequence immediately prior to the train crash places the horse's trainer, Tom Lambert, in a position to overhear Sartorys' plan. Lambert is unfortunately locked in the museum, and only just manages to escape in time to warn the horse's owner, the Marquis of Beverly, by telephone. The race against time results in Mrs Beamish, a widowed friend of Beverly's, and his granddaughter Diana, who is Lambert's love interest, saving the horse moments before the train crashes into the horse's box. In the Pimple version, the part of the hero Lambert is renamed "Lord Elpus" and played as Pimple by Fred Evans, while Mrs Beamish has become "Lady Jones" (played by Phyllis Desmond, with a turned-up putty nose and two "beauty spots"). In this version, they both visit Madame Tussaud's House of Horrors. Here the statues in the museum are explained to Lady Jane by Lord Elpus: Von Turpitz is "the man who invented turpentine"; Von Gluck is 'von o'clock, "the man who invented dinnertime". Next to a statue of the notorious murderer Charles Peace, played by an actor who keeps moving his face in a bit of comic business, is a statue of the Kaiser which causes Pimple to comment: "Fancy putting the Kaiser here, what an insult to Charles Peace!". Pimple, in an overexaggerated motion, overhears the villains plotting, and, after being released from the museum by the genie in Aladdin's lamp, effects the rescue of the horse. The following train wreck is a genuinely humorous send-up of staging special effects where the stage hands continue to get the timing wrong.

In a review of *Pimple Enlists*, *The Bioscope* noted that Pimple was an adaptable comic who could "make fun of people and of things, of ideas and of institutions". The film, a burlesque on the enlistment drives, was a potentially sensitive subject in October 1914. *The Bioscope* was able to state confidently that:

> War...is not, as a whole, a laughing matter, and it should be pointed out that Pimple's skits in connection therewith are strictly confined to such aspects of the subject as lend themselves to jesting. The jokes which this talented comedian knows so well how to crack have always been in the best of taste, and never cruel or out of place. In fact, he vies with *Punch* in the tone of his humour...Every weak spot in the enemy's armour is pierced by the keen wit of Pimple...In these sad days we have quite enough of the horrors of war in our own newspapers, if not in our lives, and there is none who will not hail with pleasure the welcome relief provided by this really clever film...There are no burlesqued war scenes. Altogether, 'Pimple Enlists' is a thoroughly wholesome and delightful little entertainment.[22]

This article not only indicates the sensitive nature of the subject of the war, but also provides a clear sense of the appeal of the Pimple films. The comparison to *Punch* is instructive, not only because it underscores the role of the wit of the intertitles in the overall humorous effect, but also because *Punch* by this time was a mainly middlebrow journal and approximated the type of audience for the Pimple films. The Evans brothers were able to work through the war period with a great degree of success. In my examination of the local exhibition practices of the cinemas in Southampton during the war, I have found that the films played consistently in the High Street cinemas, particularly those which had continuous programmes. They were also often advertised as a particular feature of the Sunday evening film shows at the MacNaughten-owned "Palace" music-hall. The significance of the High Street cinemas and the music-hall is that the audiences for these venues were drawn from a wider class base than the neighbourhood cinemas. Fred Evans supplemented his films with personal appearances at cinemas where he would perform as Pimple in-between the cinema programmes. In March 1915, he demonstrated support for the war effort by selling pictures (probably of himself as Pimple) for the "Pictures Fund" for cigarettes for "our boys at the front". On this tour, it is recorded that he played the Central Hall Wandsworth, Central Hall Norwood, and Central Hall in Inverness.[23]

As the Lydia Shroebree letter shows, his fan base included adults as well as children. Although in a humorous vein, one letter attempted to delineate the diversity of Pimple's audience:

> As I look upon the faces before me I reflect in this manner: side by side they come – the Employer and the Employee – Publican and Sinner – Mistress and Servant – Married and Unmarried (and the neutrals) – Landlords and Tennants – Policemen and ex-Convicts. There they sit. Before they entered a world of difference separated them, but now watch their faces: lit up and transformed into an expression of joy impossible to describe, see them – as they rock to and fro, convulsed with laughter; surely some miracle has taken place. You turn your eyes from the people to the screen, and Lo and behold, the explanation is simplicity itself:...that wonderful magician 'Pimple'...it is him, then, whose magnetic individuality has transformed the crowd – that has brought them all onto one level – everything is forgotten, they are all for the time being all one – for they one and all follow with sparkling eyes the one and only 'Pimple'.[24]

The wide appeal of a form of comedy based in the comic sketch and pantomime is apparent in this verbose but intriguing letter. The description in the last sentence is of a gazing audience. The films that survive, however, largely depend on an awareness of the object of the burlesque. In this regard, the audience is not a passive one, but one engaged in picking up references. The wide appeal of Pimple suggests that the combination of the sight gag and the "wit" of the intertitles also allowed multiple avenues of engagement – i.e. jokes for adults and for children. This is the technique of pantomime.

The question of how audiences made sense of the Pimple films can therefore be answered through acknowledging the traditions of the pantomime clown and the comic sketch as central to audience comprehension, as well as the use of already existing filmic structures and techniques such as those associated with the gag and the chase films. The tendency to dismiss the Pimple films in terms of their stunted cinematic development has the effect of suppressing these performance conventions, and here, in particular, it ignores the burlesque tradition. This was an approach utilised by the Evans brothers as a response to the industry trend towards feature-length narratives. It is interesting to contrast that with Chaplin's own response to these changes in his move to incorporate pathos in his comedy. This is a form of cinema which has not survived the historian's preoccupation with the development of a cinematic art, and which ignores the antecedents and continuities of other performance and entertainment traditions on which British cinema comedy undoubtedly drew. The Pimple films used a unique combination of burlesque and pantomime which was clearly flexible enough to incorporate a wide variety of subjects, from theatrical sensations to the war. Emerging out of the tradition of the comic sketch, they brought with them a broad base appeal which allowed the character of Pimple a degree of latitude in dealing with these subjects. Tailored for a British audience and supplemented by personal appearances and a regular column in the fan magazines, the Pimple films do not seem to have exported successfully. Nevertheless, they indicate a style and a mode of production which required audience interaction beyond the text. They provide an insight into the social function of the cinema, and are evidence of a comic performance tradition which continued with The Crazy Gang in the 1930s and the *Carry On* films of the 1950s and 1960s, traditions that form a central part of British film comedy.

Notes

I would like to thank Tony Fletcher and Andy Medhurst for their helpful comments and suggestions; of course, any errors are wholly mine.

[1] "Britain's Greatest Film Players", *Pictures and the Picturegoer* 8: 72 (3 July 1915): 249. Emphasis in original.

[2] Rachael Low, *The History of the British Film 1914-1918* (London: George Allen & Unwin, 1950): 167-168.

[3] Ibid: 169.

[4] John Montgomery, *Comedy Films: 1894-1954* (London: George Allen & Unwin, revised second edition, 1968): 66.

[5] Andy Medhurst, "Music Hall and British Cinema", in Charles Barr (ed), *All Our Yesterdays: 90 Years of British Cinema* (London: British Film Institute, 1986): 171.

[6] Ibid: 185.

[7] Denis Gifford interview with Joe Evans, 1966. I would like to thank Tony Fletcher for drawing my attention to this interview.

[8] "'Pimple' Past and Present: Fun and Facts Elucidated by the Editor", *Pictures and the Picturegoer* 8: 59 (3 April 1915): 9.

[9] Gifford interview.

[10] Mack Sennett, *King of Comedy: As Told to Cameron Shipp* (Garden City, New York: Doubleday & Company, 1954): 148.

[11] Montgomery: 62.

[12] Gifford interview.

[13] See Charles Musser, "Work, Ideology and Chaplin's Tramp", *Radical History Review* 41 (1988): 36-66, for a full discussion of the way in which historical context of Chaplin's tramp has been de-emphasised in favour of the tramp as "eternal clown" by film historians and critics.

[14] "'Pimple': Result of Readers' Competition", *Pictures and the Picturegoer* 19 June 1915: 216.

[15] Lois Rutherford notes two "cultural signposts": "Firstly, the antics of the pantomime clown and the pattern of construction of the harlequinade fashioned by Joey Grimaldi in [the] early nineteenth century both influenced the shape and spirit of music-hall sketches...The second signpost from the legitimate stage is theatrical farce. In this genre the characters are exaggerated and developed through their eccentricities, and unlike romantic comedy, they have little time for sentimentality in relations between the sexes". "'Harmless Nonsense': The Comic Sketch and the Development of Music-Hall Entertainment", in J S

Bratton (ed), *Music Hall: Performance and Style* (Milton Keynes; Philadelphia: Open University Press, 1986): 135, 137.

[16]   Gifford interview.

[17]   Ibid.

[18]   Kristin Thompson, *Exporting Entertainment: America in the World Film Market 1907-34* (London: British Film Institute, 1985).

[19]   Rutherford: 142-143.

[20]   "Picture Pars for Picturegoers", *Pictures and the Picturegoer* 7: 38 (7 November 1914): 190-191.

[21]   George Du Maurier, *Trilby* (London: Everyman, 1994): 14-16.

[22]   "The Pick of the Programmes. What We Think of Them: Pimple Enlists", *The Bioscope* 25: 416 (1 October 1914): 78-79.

[23]   "Pimple Pushes Pictures", *Pictures and the Picturegoer* 7: 58 (27 March 1915): 554. The fact that he appeared at "Central Halls" suggests that he was working with an exhibition chain but I have not come across any clear evidence of this.

[24]   "'Pimple': Result of Readers' Competition".

1 Florence Turner impersonating Charlie Chaplin in a publicity still

2 George Albert Smith's *The Miller and the Sweep* (1897)

3 *The Rivals – Some Chippings From the New Splinters Dancing Troupe* (c.1927)

4 *The Rivals – Some Chippings From the New Splinters Dancing Troupe* (c.1927)

5 "Found" ethnographic footage used to comic effect
in *Crossing the Great Sagrada* (1924)

6, 7 Comic juxtaposition in *Crossing the Great Sagrada* (1924)

8 American comedienne Florence Turner practising for a face-making competition in *Daisy Doodad's Dial* (1914)

9 Haunted by her facial contortions – *Daisy Doodad's Dial* (1914)

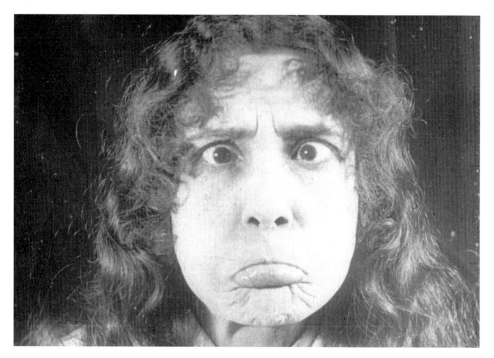

10 Close-up demonstrating Florence Turner's facial comedy
in *Daisy Doodad's Dial* (1914)

11 Graphic intertitle illustrating comic juxtaposition from *The Bump* (1920)

12, 13 Opening scene and announcement of the star in *East is East* (1916)

14 Fred Evans as Pimple in *Pimple's Wonderful Gramophone* (1913)

15 "Playing Adam's Game" from *Eve's Film Review* (1921)

16, 17 Pimple enacts his own form of censorship in *Pimple Has One* (1915)

18, 19 The influential chase comedy of Alf Collins:
The Missing Legacy; or, The Story of a Brown Hat (1906)

20, 21 Facial comedy in George Albert Smith's *The Old Maid's Valentine* (1900)

22, 23 Facial comedy in George Albert Smith's *The Old Maid's Valentine* (1900)

24 Comedian Lupino Lane in a Glasgow publicity stunt

25 1914 Pathé newsreel presenting seaside fashions

26 Douglas Fairbanks wishes Felix luck in a Pathé newsreel item,
"The Lure of the East" (c.1925)

27 Tom Green taking advantage of a close-shot in George Albert Smith's
Comic Face (1897)

28 Florence Turner impersonates the great Sarah Bernhardt
in *Film Favourites* (1914)

29 Will Kellino's parody of *Romeo and Juliet* (1915), part of a series,
Shakespeare Minced, for Cricks

30 "The Rival" from *Eve's Film Review* (1930)

31 Men in frocks: the New Splinters dancing troupe from *Eve's Film Review* (c.1927)

Weary Willie and Tired Tim Go Into Pictures: The Comic Films of the British and Colonial Kinematograph Company

Gerry Turvey

The British and Colonial Kinematograph Company (B&C) existed from 1908 to 1924, but its most interesting period of operation was from autumn 1909 to summer 1916.[1] During these years, the company was recognised in the film trade press and beyond as a lively and progressive producer, one of Britain's leading firms, and an important contributor to Britain's expanding film industry.[2]

Yet, the cinema was only the latest phase in the steady growth of an urban-commercial culture that had been developing since the 1830s. Initially, popular fictions and theatrical melodramas had been established for the new urban working class. These were joined by the music-halls in the 1850s, and then, in the 1890s, by the mass publication of magazines, newspapers and comics. B&C was deeply rooted within this culture, and functioned in terms of interdependence and exchange with it. So, for example, early company personnel were drawn from the realms of the music-hall and the circus. The firm established links with Alfred Harmsworth's *The Daily Mail, Evening News* and his comic paper *Illustrated Chips*. Furthermore, the popular magazine *Pearson's Weekly*, one of Harmsworth's rivals, provided the stories for B&C's film series about the Spanish bandit Don Q (released throughout 1913), while, in return, B&C's highly popular film series starring Lieutenant Daring became a regular short story feature in *Pearson's Magazine* from September 1912.

"Variety" seems to have been the master *form* across all these popular media, and provided the format for the halls, pantomime and even melodrama, for periodicals such as *Tit-Bits* and *Pearson's Magazine*, for the comic papers, and for early cinema performances. B&C initially served the latter by turning out a range of films from topicals and actualities, through short dramas to comic films. However, between 1909 and 1916, that programming variety began to be displaced by the development of the longer feature "exclusives" that served to redefine the cinema-going experience. Hence, the intermittent variety package of lower-class culture gave way to the sustained narrative dramas of a more bourgeois culture. Consequently, from mid-1914, established novels and plays increasingly provided the stories for B&C films and their last comic was released in July 1915.

My contention is that their early films, and especially the comics, were part of the vulgar popular entertainments that catered for lower-middle-class and working-class audiences, and that the company drew on resources from within that culture to help in the establishment of its new filmmaking practices. More specifically, I am proposing that there was a direct transfer of the imaginative world and its modes of visual representation *from* the mass-circulation comic papers *to* the film comics. George Perry has suggested that a "golden age" of British comics ran from the turn of the century until late in the First World War, and this period, of course, directly coincided with the emergence of cinema in Britain and with its search for viable film forms.[3]

The film comic stayed short. Thus, at B&C, its average length in 1909 was 333', and this had risen to only 643' by 1914, whereas the company's dramas, which began at an average length of 590' in 1909, rapidly grew to 2040' in 1914, and 3763' in 1916. This brevity was because the *comic* film was a distinctive narrative form, closely related to popular culture's comic strips, and so different in kind from the more extended narratives of the theatrical *comedies* and dramas associated with the middle classes. It was a form constrained to make its impact in a short time and via a limited number of shots. Nevertheless, by 1915, several film periodicals had grown restive with this form,[4] and, in 1948, Rachael Low accused the early comic film of, in effect, a lack of narrative ambition.[5] But this was to miss the point, for such commentators were approaching the comics from an unsympathetic position which favoured cause and effect narration and those forms, such as "comedy" and "the novel", esteemed by respectable culture. In the longer run, this position gained the ascendancy but, for a while, an alternative and disrespectful form delighted popular audiences.

A marked continuity runs from the magazine comics that appeared in the 1890s, through the British comic films of the pre-war years, and on to the comic paper *Film Fun* in the 1920s. Initially, the films drew from the periodicals, whereas *Film Fun* drew from both the earlier papers and the film comedians of the 1910s. Essentially, however, both media occupied the same social and moral universe, and deployed similar visual and narrative conventions.

Thus, from the outset, the comic films adopted their generic name from the comic papers, and were released and identified in sales catalogues and the trade press as "comics". Furthermore, given their initial success, in the summer of 1910, B&C proposed to increase their comic output in order to release a film each week. This would have allowed them to match the weekly periodicity of the comic papers.[6] They never did realise this aspiration, and, out of a total comic output of 98 films between 1908 and 1915, their best years were 1914, with 24 comics released, 1911 with twenty, and 1915 with nineteen.[7]

B&C also seem to have taken their cue from the magazine comics when they thought in terms of having particular characters appear regularly over a series of issues. But, yet again, this plan was not well-sustained. During the initial drive to establish the company, a tramp called Drowsy Dick – a direct descendant of Dreamy Daniel from the comic paper *Lot-o'-Fun*, begun in 1906 – was to form a series, but only two films were made. Similarly, only a couple of films each appeared featuring the inept middle-class husband "Gilbert" and the hapless Bliggs family. There was a more sustained series of four films in 1914 featuring the Hurricanes – three incorrigible children who would wreak havoc wherever they went. They were the heirs of "The Ball's Pond Road Banditti", the disruptive shop boys who had appeared in *Larks* in 1893, and they provided a good example of what Davison, B&C's agent, promoted as "those riotous, terrible children pictures".[8] There were also four films in the summer of 1911 featuring Weary Willie and Tired Tim from *Illustrated Chips* that proved a "phenomenal success" for the company.[9] Alongside these characters was "Snorky". He was William Gladstone Haley, one of the four B&C players sufficiently well-known and popular in 1914 to have his picture issued by the company in a series of postcards.[10] Haley specialised in comic films, and regularly figured in them in his comic persona of "Snorky", thereby giving some sense of continuity to the company's product analogous to the regular characters of the magazines.[11]

Both magazines and films also featured a comic universe made up of a particular physical environment inhabited by a range of distinctive "social types".

In his "anatomy" of *Film Fun* magazine, Graham King characterised its late realisation. For him, "the environment depicted...[was] an urban working class district" whose visual representation had been simplified and stereotyped into a handful of elements.[12] Essentially, these were terraced housing, a kerbed pavement with its street furniture of bollards and lamp-posts, and the railway viaduct archway. This urban district is also that of the B&C comics. Filmed in East Finchley and Walthamstow, London's pavements and terraces provide the locations for films in which there is a regular movement from interiors out onto the urban streets where a multiplication of troublesome incidents can occur. Hence, in *Playing Truant* (July 1910), Bobby, the mischievous schoolboy, leaves his comfortable bourgeois home to upset whomever he meets in the local roads. King also noted the significance of building sites, scaffolding and mortar, and these, too, offer opportunities for humour in a number of the B&C films. Finally, he emphasised the importance for comic business of those doors and windows that open directly onto the street. Here, too, B&C had anticipated the magazine's approach, as when Willie and Tim first spy their prize in *The Plum Pudding Stakes* (April 1911).

This urban scene was also peopled by various standard urban types who could be the recipients of the protagonists' trickery and comic violence. B&C's films therefore present the viewer with shopkeepers and delivery men, costers and billposters, sweeps and dustmen, building workers and policemen. The latter figure in film after film. In *Film Fun*, King found that they were depicted as greedy and dishonest, and as a violent, unpredictable enemy. Aspects of the magazine's anti-authoritarian tone have their equivalent in the B&C comics, as when Snorky, in the popular *The Butler's Revenge* (released July 1910 and reissued December 1912), dresses in his rival's police uniform in order to cause various people inconvenience, before returning the costume and allowing an irate crowd to vent their anger on the policeman. Rarely in the films are the police a source of reassurance. In contrast, tramps are privileged figures, their depredations licensed by the tremendous popularity of their original models in *Chips*, Weary Willie and Tired Tim.

Comic films such as those of B&C seem also to have derived elements of their technique from the magazine strips. The latter, it should be noted, were themselves a relatively new form. *Funny Folks* first established the variety layout for the British comic in 1874, while *Illustrated Bits* introduced the next innovation in 1885 by running a competition for "six small comic *tableaux* illustrating a *story*".[13] This brought the comic strip into the magazines and did so by evoking a term also used in the theatre for those occasions when performers would hold certain expressive gestures to reinforce the significance of a particular dramatic development. Such moments of stasis might easily be transferred to the graphic medium of the comics, and these, in turn, took on a more dynamic aspect when the comic frame was reconstituted as the film shot. Furthermore, this exchange benefitted from a key event in the history of the comic papers. The artist Tom Browne created "the true British comic style" when he first drew Weary Willie and Tired Tim for *Illustrated Chips* in May 1896.[14] That paper followed *Funny Folks* by offering four pages of stories, series and serials in text and a jumble of jokes and strips on its back and centre pages. Browne's originality lay in his conceiving the six-panel, full-page strip for the cover and providing a highly influential narrative model for other magazine artists and for the makers of comic films. B&C were therefore selecting the most "progressive" aspect of the comic papers' design when they adopted Willie and Tim in 1911.

Denis Gifford has observed that clearly ruled frames, such as those used by Browne, were not common before 1898, but that, thereafter, a standard comic style developed made up of "clean, neat, open line work spotted with well-balanced blacks, plus plenty of action. Action, simple slapstick in pictures: this was the *completely new thing* comics had to offer."[15] This style was well-illustrated in "A Wild Night's Adventure with Spring-Heeled Jack" from 9 September 1899, in which fat Tim dressed as another famous figure from popular culture to scare farm labourers, policemen and, through their window, a domestic couple, before coming to grief as the elements of a chase appeared in the background of the final panel.[16] It was this technique of narration via tableaux that could be adopted by the early comic films, and this borrowing can be illustrated through a comparison between a *Chips'* strip for 21 December 1918[17] and B&C's *The Plum Pudding Stakes* released April 1911. The similarities prove particularly close.

Firstly, the strip uses just twelve frames to tell its story, while the four-minute film is accomplished in only nineteen shots (it lacks its intertitles). Secondly, the strip is made up of three episodes: an incident with a hoop and a policeman; breaking into a room for a meal; and the pair's discovery hiding behind a map. Similarly, the film offers three events: Willie, Tim and their dog steal from a butcher's boy; they then disrupt a Punch and Judy show and are chased; finally, they steal a plum pudding. Finally, both strip and film carefully detail the mechanics of illegal acts: the strip uses four frames to illustrate how a cane and a Christmas pudding can be used for breaking and entering, while the film uses an alternating sequence of five shots to demonstrate how to steal a plum pudding.

Thus, a clear system of exchanges was operating between the fields of magazine and film comedy. With the one, a series of well-organised graphic frames, and, with the other, a succession of well-chosen film shots provided comparable visual techniques for the construction of that sequence of significant tableaux necessary to sustain a brief, but coherent, comic narrative.

However, these narratives had their own distinct construction which was an intermittent and episodic one, rather than a logically developing sequence of cause-and-effect. Many of B&C's early comics deployed an *additive* narrative structure where outrageous event was added to event in a series, and a picaresque succession of mishaps, violence and knockabout developed. Contemporary insight into this method was provided in *The Film House Record*'s description of *A Cheap Removal* (August 1910) as "a really funny comic containing a *continuous series* of amusing and laughable *incidents* of a very characteristic nature".[18] So, for example, in *Playing Truant*, Bobby first pushes over a policeman and then progresses by splashing a billposter with paste, turning the paste pail over a black man's head, tumbling a building worker into mortar, pulling the cloth off a table, tying a smoke bomb to an artist's coat, thrusting a fisherman into a pond, and collapsing a tent onto a group of scouts. Similarly, Papa Huggins, in his pageant costume as *The Prehistoric Man* (January 1911), is first hustled by a park-keeper, then he upsets a costermonger, bumps into sandwich-board men, is covered with refuse while hiding in a dustcart, and is finally captured on a building site. These event series regularly develop into a chase which – besides its function in early film form of binding together a succession of shots – offers an opportunity to aggregate the injured and insulted citizenry into a vengeful crowd.

By 1914, a second category of comic film was being developed by B&C. This also avoided conventional narrative development, since these films hinged upon the creation of a difficult or embarrassing *situation* for one of the characters. Thus, in *Two Sides to a Boat* (December 1913), a suffragette hiding from a pursuing crowd is outraged when she thinks she overhears two old sailors preparing to tar her all over and, in *A Pleasant Way to Get Thin* (April 1914), a husband is embarrassed when his wife and daughter surprise him wearing a dance skirt at a girls' ballet academy.

These two narrative strategies are, in turn, associated with various recurrent "themes", the most common of which is that of *social disruption*. In film after film, everyday routine is disturbed by unsettling and often violent intrusions. Thus, in *The Plum Pudding Stakes*, Willie and Tim upset conventional domesticity when they steal the pudding, and cause havoc in the street when they interrupt the Punch and Judy show. In *What Happened to the Dog's Medicine* (June 1910), Jones treats ice cream with the animal's medicine and all who eat it go down on all fours, bark and bite. Furthermore, once a process of disruption has been launched, it is followed through to a conclusion, the disruptions moving the comedy forward. Sometimes, the films close on retribution for the disruptive transgressor – as when Bobby in *Playing Truant* is thrown into the pond by his pursuers – but often they do not. Thus, *A Cheap Removal* ends on a scene of devastation, and "the last we see is a mass of writhing people, broken furniture, destroyed bedding and flying feathers".[19] Even then, retribution seems to gesture towards conventional morality in rather a perfunctory manner – Willie and Tim are apprehended by the police at only the very last moment – and the pleasure on offer is largely to be derived from the transgressions, disruptions and mayhem upon which the films dwell.

A second and equally pervasive comic theme involves trickery and the use of "smartness", ingenuity and pranks to gain an advantage over others. In *A Deal in Crockery* (released May 1910; reissued September 1912), Snorky and Nobbler, having acquired some broken china, lay it out beside an overturned barrow to make sympathy collections from kindly passers-by; they then double their deceit by selling the "business" to another couple who, unfortunately, get found out. Likewise, in *How Mickey Dooley Survived the Coal Strike*, a topical comic issued during the strike of May 1912, the jobless Mickey, sitting in his garden, is pelted with coal by bargees unloading their cargo; as a consequence, he and his son contrive a dummy that is subsequently showered with enough coal for them to sell it off profitably the next morning, dressed in the height of fashion – an episode that could equally have appeared in the comic papers. As with the agents of disruption, tricksters, too, are sometimes punished, but are more often left unscathed. So, after sticking up various people in *Marie's Joke with the Fly Papers* (November 1910), the guilty child escapes chastisement as the outraged populace tape up the innocent vendor of the papers, and, in *Quits* (July 1911), a young gentleman, who has surprised and seen off a burglar robbing a library, himself takes the spoils, only to have the first thief follow him and successfully steal the loot back.

A third regular comic theme – often combined with trickery – is that of *revenge*. Thus, in *The Tables Turned* (October 1910), a dwarf, dressed as a baby in order to beg dishonestly, is "kidnapped" by tramps who disguise themselves as a woman and a blind man to use "baby", in turn, for begging; but the dwarf contrives to turn the tables, grab the money and cause the pair to be exposed, chased and captured. In *The Artist's Ruse* (released January 1911 and reissued March 1913), the painter, in revenge for a rich customer spying on his female assistant through a telescope, casts shadows onto a blind which seem to suggest that he has just stabbed her; customer and police follow the "assassin" transporting a body, only to be dumbfounded when they discover it is an artist's model figure.

Furthermore, underpinning these themes and narratives is a distinctive, non-standard morality. In his analysis of *Film Fun*, Graham King contended that the "content of many of its stories and strips was...morally dubious, chauvinistic and bigoted. It projected a tone of passive subversion, which gives a clue to its immense popularity."[20] He listed several moral positions presented in the paper, many of which had already been prefigured in the B&C films and, before that, in the worlds inhabited by Willie and Tim. Thus, "crime can pay", especially theft, and rogues often get away with it, as when the cunning dwarf in *The Tables Turned* prospers and the first burglar in *Quits* reassumes his stolen bounty. Similarly, "finders keepers" is not challenged, and so the father in *When the Pie Was Opened*

(April 1915), who sees a sack of flour fall from a miller's cart, unashamedly retains it to cook a huge pie for his family. Furthermore, "cheating is clever" and acceptable, provided it is conducted with ingenuity. Dextrous trickery is one of the most common themes in the B&C films, and cons, schemes and chicanery are carried out with impunity by both the respectable and ruffianly, and are celebrated for their inventiveness. Finally, "revenge is sweet", as well as being a common justification for petty crime and an unsanctioned response to those who have deceived, hurt or stolen from a comic protagonist. Revenge was a standard theme for B&C films and could be linked with undeserved rewards for trickery. Thus, in *His Maiden Aunt* (May 1913), Freddy Fritters dresses as a rich aunt of the Mann household in order to play tricks on them out of revenge; later, thinking she is him, they abuse the real aunt who disinherits them for Freddy.

In many ways, these moral stances are favourable to the dispossessed and needy, and the dimension of "passive subversion" is undoubtedly integral to them, for the B&C comic world divides clearly between "them" and "us". "They" are associated with prosperity, middle-class propriety, meanness and established authority, whereas the "we" perspective adopted by the films is associated with anti-authoritarianism, "redistribution", quick-wittedness, irreverence and high spirits. Thus, the B&C comics regularly celebrate the more liberatory and provocative aspects of the lively vulgar culture that had been consolidating within the urban working class over the previous decades. The comics – until they were ousted from the production schedules in 1915 by the longer middle-class dramas – were therefore an integral part of a commercial popular culture still responsive to the urban experience of its lower-class audience, and to the more subversive elements in its alternative value system.

Notes

[1]   This essay is part of a larger investigation of the B&C Company, its films and personnel, and constitutes only a part of my account of their comic output.

[2]   *Pictures and the Picturegoer* printed a series on "Birthplaces of British Films". The first three articles dealt with Hepworth 6: 14 (23 May 1914): 320-322; the London Film Company 6: 16 (6 June 1914): 366-368; and the British and Colonial Film Company 6: 19 (27 June 1914): 426-428, and 6: 20 (4 July 1914): 444-445, 458. There had also been an earlier item on B&C: 1: 4 (1 November 1913): 99-104, 124.

[3]   George Perry and Alan Aldridge, *The Penguin Book of Comics: A slight history*, revised edition (London: Penguin Books, 1971).

[4]   See, for example, A Christie, "The Making of a Good Film Comedy", *The Kinematograph & Lantern Weekly* 434: 19 (19 August 1915): 12-13, and "The Comic Film", *The Picture Palace News* 22 November 1915: 63.

[5]   Rachael Low, *The History of the British Film 1906-1914* (London: George Allen & Unwin, 1949): 168-169.

[6]   See "The Butler's Revenge", *The Film House Record* 16 (25 June 1910): 138; "Wanted, a Bath Chair Attendant", *The Film House Record* 17 (9 July 1910): 155; and *The Kinematograph & Lantern Weekly* 14 July 1910.

[7]   There were only four comics each in 1908 and 1909.

[8]   See Davison's advertisement for *Two Little Angels* (July 1914) in *The Kinematograph & Lantern Weekly* 28 May 1914: 28.

[9]   See Cosmopolitan's advertisement in *The Kinematograph & Lantern Weekly* 20 April 1911.

[10]   See *Pictures and the Picturegoer* 6: 8 (11 April 1914).

[11]   See "The Adventures of 'Snorky'", *The Pictures* 28 December 1912: 12.

[12]   Graham King, *The Wonderful World of Film Fun: The Comic Anatomy of Film Fun 1920-1962* (London: Clarkes New Press, 1985): 16.

[13]   Quoted in Denis Gifford, *Victorian Comics* (London: George Allen & Unwin, 1976): 9. Emphases added.

[14]   Denis Gifford, "Comics of the Great War", in *Great Newspapers Reprinted: Six Comics of World War One* (London: Peter Way, 1972): 2.

[15]   Gifford (1976): 24. Emphasis added.

[16]   Reproduced in ibid: 29.

[17]   Reproduced in Gifford (1972).

[18]   "A Cheap Removal", *The Film House Record* 6 August 1910: 173. Emphasis added.

[19]   "A Cheap Removal", *The Kinematograph & Lantern Weekly* 25 August 1910: 1049.

[20]   King: 119.

"My career up to now":[1] Betty Balfour and the Background to the *Squibs* Series

Judith McLaren

In February 1924, the popular journal *The Referee* ran a competition offering its readers the chance to come up with an idea for a new film story featuring the popular British film star Betty Balfour.[2] The competition coincided with the release of *Squibs MP* (1924), the latest film from the small but critically respected company of Welsh-Pearson, featuring Balfour as Piccadilly flower-seller Amelia "Squibs" Hopkins, and shortly to be followed by the final film in the series, *Squibs Honeymoon* (1924).[3] It was clearly designed as a promotional stunt, urging hopeful competitors to "see these films, study the character of Miss Balfour...and *begin your story at once*",[4] and featured weekly box advertisements, listing where the films were currently playing.

Behind this, however, there also appears to have been a genuine desire to uncover new ideas, and *The Referee* quickly began to express its dissatisfaction with its readers' suggestions, most of which derived from literary classics. "Please do not suggest that Miss Balfour would act well as Little Nell, Dora, Rosalind, Dolly Varden, Beatrice or Becky Sharpe, or any such well-known character", the organisers complained. "Think out some original incident, humorous or dramatic, in which a clever film actress such as Miss Balfour would take the chief part. It is not difficult. Hundreds of quaint and interesting things are happening around us everyday."[5] By March, their tone had become exasperated, rejecting, among other things, yet more characters from English classics and well-known plays, and "stories with Betty Balfour featuring as a gypsy queen or Spanish dancer".[6] Most insistently, *The Referee* refused to countenance any suggestion that Balfour continue with the further adventures of "Squibs".

Thomas Welsh, who produced the *Squibs* films, expressed some sympathy with the public's disappointment: "it is an astonishing fact that in the many thousands of letters 'our Betty' receives from all parts of the world, one question is always asked. When will the next *Squibs* picture be ready? And there is no doubt that millions of fans will be disappointed when they learn that *Squibs Honeymoon* is to be the last of the series".[7] *The Motion Picture Studio*, however, consoled itself for the loss of this particular character by considering that, after all, "'Squibs' is so much Betty Balfour that in a sense we may be said to have her with us still".[8]

The *Squibs* films are fascinating for many reasons – not just as popular comedies which engage with contemporary discourses of class, nationality and gender, and which were successful both in the home market and overseas, but also as examples of a remarkable creative partnership between Balfour and director George Pearson which lasted for six years and twelve films, and established the actress as Britain's leading film comedienne. Contemporary critics compared Balfour's screen personality to Mary Pickford[9] and Charlie Chaplin;[10] later writers have seen her as a forerunner to Gracie Fields,[11] and the films' success came at a time when the British film industry was re-examining its attitude towards "stars" and the "star system". The way in which the films both shape, and are shaped by, their star performer exemplifies the shifting strategies adopted by an independent filmmaking firm of the period. The competition cited above, for instance, was part of a vast campaign by Gaumont, which had taken over the rights to Welsh-Pearson's films from Jury in the previous year, to "boom" Balfour on an unprecedented scale as a British film star able to compete with the Americans.[12] Moving from sentimental comedy to melodrama and slapstick farce, the *Squibs* films illustrate the full range of Balfour's performance styles at the start of her career, and they consolidated a screen image whose popular appeal and commercial significance were neatly summed up by a fan's "Kinema Carol":

> 'Highbrows' and 'lowbrows' for once must agree
> That everything charming commencing with 'B'
> British, Blonde, Bonnie, Bewitching and more
> Can be said in two little words Betty Balfour.
> Dear little 'Squibs,' has it dawned on you yet
> That you're England's 'White Hope'
> and Welsh-Pearson's best Bet?[13]

This essay is part of a larger consideration of the *Squibs* series, and offers a brief outline of the artistic context from which Balfour's characterisation emerged.

Although Balfour is frequently paired with Ivor Novello, in terms of her success as a British star during the 1920s, she is generally offered as a contrast to the actor who came to pictures as an established theatrical star.[14] This is to underestimate the extent of Balfour's performing experience and reputation before she entered films. She began as a society entertainer while still a child, and moved rapidly onto the London stage, working for Fred Karno and C B Cochran, appearing in her own revue turn, and shifting gradually towards more mainstream drama after the end of the war.

Her first film appearance was in *Nothing Else Matters* (1920).[15] Accounts of what drew her to Welsh-Pearson's notice vary, but in 1951, in an early version of the autobiographical material that was to become his memoir, *Flashback* (1957), Pearson noted that Balfour's talent was immediately obvious, and "her part developed accordingly".[16] Pearson's project for the film was ambitious: the characters and story – a music-hall comic's declining fortunes drive him into jealousy and temporary madness, and almost cause the loss of his wife and child – were designed to offer different perspectives on "the eternal search for happiness",[17] and both structure and treatment played extensively with different notions of fact and fiction, tragedy and comedy, performance and reality.

Balfour's role, Sally, the stock "Mary Jane" character of a comical skivvy, generally functions according to convention, rather than individuality. She sticks loyally by her employer through thick and thin, a faithful, if incompetent, retainer. Her fanatical dedication to cheap romances leads her to neglect housework and botch cookery, before ultimately striking a more serious note, when she allows the hero's infant son to wander off to an initially uncertain fate.

Pearson developed the role to allow Balfour to demonstrate her ability to play both ends of the scale, tragic and comic. Her comic performance is generally presented in continuous, full-length shots, which emphasise it as a comic turn, with her waddling walk, bulky costume, ungainly posture, and constant gestures and grimaces. Much of the comedy is played out front, and Sally often addresses the audience directly, sometimes mouthing comments clearly designed to be lip-read.

During the tragic section, Balfour appears to shift into a more conventionally histrionic mode, which produces a slight alteration in presentation. Besides full-length shots which depict her running agitatedly around, hair streaming, and all comic gestural mannerisms temporarily abandoned, there is an insert medium-shot, later repeated, taken discontinuously against a blank background, and strongly side-lit. In this shot, she rears back from the camera, clutching her hands to the side of her head, face aghast, before rushing off right. Again, the moment is directed straight at the audience, and there is a clear contrast between the relative intimacy of this shot and the film's more distanced depiction of the central character's madness and misery, which is generally presented in tableaux. The effect in both comic and tragic modes is an abrupt break with the film's prevailing modes, an emphasis on performance as much as the emotion performed, and the establishment of a close relationship between Balfour's character and the audience.

Equally, while the intertitles concerning the central characters are often in third-person narrative or commentary, Balfour's intertitles invariably function as direct speech, rendered emphatic with italics and capitals, dropped aitches, phonetics, and slang expressions. Many of her remarks are purely comic, relying upon the contrast between her expression, syntax and pronunciation, and conventional speech – although during one tragic scene in which she comforts the hero's grief-stricken wife, she lapses into standard English: again, the effect is to open a dialogue with the audience and their expectations, often quite literally.

Pearson hoped that Balfour would offer the audience a way into the film, earthing the more artistic or melodramatic sequences.[18] Throughout the film, she plays an increasingly choric function, her constant comparisons between real life and fiction both framing and puncturing the central action; and, by the end of the film, having covered the extremes of comedy and tragedy, both character and performance stabilise in a mode which is very close to the style which Balfour adopts in the *Squibs* films. In the final scene, besides taking a couple of expert pratfalls in an unfamiliar pastoral setting, she is firmly established as the audience's route into the film: her gaze coordinates and anchors the various lovers' reunions, as their embraces are intercut with head-and-shoulder shots of her watching, and smiling approvingly, no longer grotesque or clad in her skivvy costume, but conventionally attractive and made-up, like a cross between Puck and Cupid.

Given the way in which this closing scene is structured, it was almost inevitable that the trade show audience should respond warmly to Balfour's performance.[19] Critical appraisals generally identified it as rather at odds with Pearson's artistic ambitions, while being reflective of his authorial weakness for theatrical convention (although it is arguable that his use of it was deliberate and reflexive).[20] It was also suggested that Balfour's exuberant performance, with its mixture of pathos and low comedy – particularly the latter – would be largely responsible for the film's success with audiences.[21]

Next, Pearson tried Balfour out in a more serious role, as *Mary-Find-the-Gold* (1922), the story of a country girl coming to grief in the big city. Although he and the trade press conceded that the characterisation did not allow her to demonstrate her comic talents as *Nothing Else Matters* had done,[22] the synopsis indicates several scenes of drama and pathos, conveyed largely through tableaux or stoic impassivity, as opposed to the rapid movement, fragmentation and gesture of her first film.[23] This suggests how her performance style was evolving with Pearson, whose theories of screenacting at this time were particularly concerned with establishing a mode of performance sufficiently removed from theatrical convention on the one hand, and naturalism on the other, to strip a dramatic performance to the bare minimum of gesture and expression, in order to stimulate the audience's imagination to supply the requisite emotion and feeling.

Besides drama and pathos, *Mary-Find-the-Gold* included scenes which made a feature of Balfour dancing – in this case, privately in her humble garret. Her dance is seen here primarily as an expression of innocent pleasure, and the audience's "innocent" pleasure in it as spectacle is explicitly contrasted with the image of dance as a social, sexualised ritual in the scene which follows. The image, and contrast, recurs with different inflections through several of Balfour's films – for instance, with a comic inflection in *Love, Life and Laughter* (1923), and in the opening sequence of *Squibs* (1922). But ultimately, and in contrast to her later films which focus on independent, self-sufficient heroines, *Mary-Find-the-Gold* takes a punitive approach to its central character's desire to succeed in obtaining riches through her own efforts. Her naïvety and folly lead to her imprisonment, from which her fiancé finally rescues her, achieving promotion for his pains. With seemingly unconscious irony, the film paints its heroine as living up to her name only through her incompetence in doing so.

"Living up to her name" was the main impetus behind scriptwriter Eliot Stannard's suggestion that Welsh-Pearson purchase the rights to Clifford Seyler's one-act play *Squibs* as a more suitable vehicle for Balfour's comic talents – the title immediately, as Pearson put it, hinting at "fireworks".[24] First performed in Brighton in 1910,[25] the play was not seen in London until June 1915, when actress Mabel Russell and her company performed it as part of the bill at Stoll's London Coliseum.[26] Although Welsh-Pearson bought, and used, nothing more than the play's name, there are clear parallels between the film and its source, in particular the theatrical tradition of cockney representation from which it derived, and its impact on both Balfour's and Russell's careers.

The play's cockney character is rooted in the conflation of coster and cockney music-hall traditions established by Albert Chevalier in the 1890s. Chevalier's characterisations were "elaborately built up impersonations... imaginative rather than investigative...a typology rather than a sociology of London life",[27] with their roots in literary and theatrical tradition. Chevalier's artistic credo was "always keep to that little bit of human nature in your work".[28] The results, while relishing the exterior details which distinguished "them" from "us" – speech patterns, dress, gesture, milieu – also insisted on "our" common humanity, as Chevalier emphasised the "unity which underlay difference, in focusing on the universal and incarnating it in the hopes and fears of the humble coster".[29] This tradition of representation carries over into film depictions of cockney characters, not least through Chevalier's own film versions of his stage act, and there are many similarities between the critical evaluation of his work and that accorded to Balfour's performances as "Squibs".

Peckham-born Mabel Russell had first been cast as a cockney by Sir Herbert Beerbohm Tree in 1913. Although the audience was reportedly "startled" by a female character who swore and used coarse language, the latter was a consistent element of such characterisations and clearly part of their appeal. In later years, Russell claimed that she had been Tree's first choice for Eliza Doolittle.[30] *Squibs* followed instead. Russell continued to be associated with cockney parts, and in 1916 even played a French coquette as a cockney, to some acclaim. Critics described her as "a little bundle of sparks radiating over the footlights, singing, prancing, laughing, larking, as if acting were all play and no work"[31] – phrases which recur almost verbatim in responses to Balfour. Russell continued to tour with *Squibs*, as far north as Manchester (where she was mobbed by a claque of gallery girls), and even as late as 1929 she was still reviving the character, despite a significant shift in career when she replaced her husband as Conservative candidate for Berwick-upon-Tweed, and in May 1923, in circumstances curiously echoing the plot of *Squibs MP* (and duly exploited in publicity) became only the second female MP, holding the seat until the end of the decade.

In conclusion, therefore, with *Squibs* Welsh-Pearson had purchased a combination of several elements: a proven vehicle for a particular type of young and vivacious actress, which brought with it a tradition of cockney representation, a peculiar sort of imaginative realism, combined with an emphasis on skilful performance, allowing for a blend of comedy, pathos, entertainment and reflection rooted in individual character, but with guaranteed universal resonance, and an appeal to all classes of audience. The experience of two previous films together had consolidated Pearson's and Balfour's working relationship, and each had clearly contributed to the other's creative development. The impact of *Squibs'* success upon their careers, and the creative and institutional context within which they functioned, were unquestionable: nevertheless, as I hope this essay has suggested, there was little that was haphazard or fortuitous about this success. The *Squibs* series as it developed was a careful attempt to combine a range of elements in order to reap clear commercial but, equally importantly, creative benefits.

Notes

[1] Betty Balfour, "Mainly About Me", *The Picturegoer* 2: 10 (October 1921): 22-23.

[2] *The Referee* 17 February 1924: 5.

[3] The other films in the series are *Squibs* and *Squibs Wins the Calcutta Sweep* (both 1922).

[4] *The Referee* 17 February 1924: 5.

[5] *The Referee* 2 March 1924: 5.

[6] *The Referee* 9 March 1924: 5.

[7] *Film Renter* 5 January 1924: 8.

[8] *The Motion Picture Studio* (15 December 1923): 11.

[9] *Film Renter* 2 June 1923: 44.

[10] *Daily News* (29 September 1922), quoted in an advertisement for *Squibs Wins the Calcutta Sweep* in *Kinematograph Weekly* 5 October 1922: 5.

[11] John Caughie, biographical entry in Ginette Vincendeau (ed), *Encyclopedia of European Cinema* (London: Cassell/British Film Institute, 1995): 25.

[12] *Film Renter* 2 June 1923: 12.

[13] "Kinema Carols", *Pictures* 24: 417 (April 1922): 52.

[14] For example, John Russell Taylor and John Kobal, *Portraits of the British Cinema: 60 Glorious Years 1925-1985* (London: Aurum Press, 1985): 8.

[15] All references which follow are to the viewing print in the National Film and Television Archive (NFTVA).

[16] George Pearson, "Memories...", *The Cine Technician* 17: 92 (September-October 1951): 145.

[17] George Pearson, foreword for the first trade show, in the George Pearson Collection at the British Film Institute, Item 12: 90.

[18] George Pearson, *Flashback: The Autobiography of a British Film-maker* (London: George Allen & Unwin, 1957): 88.

[19] Ibid: 90.

[20] "'Nothing Else Matters'", *The Bioscope* 44: 720 (29 July 1920): 46-47.

[21]   "'Mary-Find-the-Gold'", *Kinematograph Weekly* 42: 693 (5 August 1920): 58.

[22]   Pearson (1957): 94; *The Bioscope* 44: 755 (31 March 1921): 61-62.

[23]   *Girls' Cinema* 4: 81 (29 April 1922): 3-6.

[24]   Pearson (1957): 95. Stannard became a regular collaborator with Hitchcock in the 1920s: see Charles Barr, *English Hitchcock* (Moffat: Cameron & Hollis, 1999).

[25]   Allardyce Nicoll, *English Drama 1900-1930: The Beginnings of the Modern Period* (Cambridge: Cambridge University Press, 1973): 939.

[26]   Clare Colvin (ed), *London Coliseum – Calendar* (unpublished manuscript held at the Theatre Museum, London).

[27]   Gareth Stedman Jones, "The 'cockney' and the nation, 1780-1988", in David Feldman and Gareth Stedman Jones (eds), *Metropolis London: Histories and representations since 1800* (London; New York: Routledge, 1989): 298, 300.

[28]   Ibid: 299.

[29]   Ibid: 301.

[30]   Lucy M Grimes, *The Life-story of Mabel Russell* (unpublished manuscript, held in the Theatre Museum, London): 30.

[31]   Ibid: 37.

Wit and the Literate Image:
The Adrian Brunel/A A Milne Collaborations

Christine Gledhill

This essay comes out of a long-term project to re-evaluate the British cinema of the 1920s. A major focus of such a project must be the rethinking of those categories used to condemn British cinema then and now: theatricality, pictorialism and literariness. My starting premise is that, since cinema is a heterogeneous medium capable, like the Bakhtinian novel, of ingesting and rendering all others, there is no reason *per se* why cinema should not be theatrical, pictorial or literary. The issue in the case of British cinema is to discern how these combinations might work as part of an indigenous style of, or orientation towards, filmmaking.

Here, therefore, I am concerned with "literariness", commonly rejected for its association with literary adaptation and a preponderance of literary speech in the form of intertitles or dialogue. In order to re-evaluate this association, I want to explore the productivity of "literariness" through a particular focus on the relationship between witty intertitle and image in the Brunel/A A Milne short comedies produced by Minerva Films, the company they set up in 1920 with Leslie Howard. Given the space available here, my examination will concentrate on *The Bump* (1920). This little comedy, the second in the series, concerns an upper-middle-class family and the romance between bright young "twenty somethings" Lilian, their daughter, and dreamy but ever-hopeful Freddie Fane. Lilian disdains the dancing, jazzing Freddie in her dream of a "real man", personified by John Brice, "the Great Explorer", in whose book, *Through Trackless Paths*, she is currently engrossed. As it happens, he is a guest at a fancy dress ball to which she and Freddie kindly escort her parents. Lilian is entranced by his tales, ignoring Freddie who is reduced to playing Bridge with her mother and father. After explaining that his capacity to navigate the jungles of Africa is down to his unusually enlarged "bump of locality", Brice, shorn of his train of bearers, is helplessly lost as he tries to find his way from his lodgings to 24 Stucoway Terrace, where he is invited to tea. Freddie's persistence is finally rewarded as Lilian falls tearfully into his comforting arms, while John Brice arrives at last, three months late, just in time to encounter the couple leaving for their honeymoon.

The "literariness" of this light-hearted tale emerges from the combination of witty intertitle and illustrative – literate – image. Here are the first titles, which structure the opening ten minutes of the film. Brief indications of image are given in italics.

1   Lilian Montrevor...Faith Celli (*the actress bows, smiling to us*)
2   Better take another look at her as she's the heroine.
3   John Brice, the Great Explorer...Aubrey Smith (*he gazes sternly in profile off left*)

4   Explanations of John Brice's face (*written on luggage labels attached to different parts of his face*):
     - argument with a leopard
     - battle with a scorpion in Africa
     - shark bite in Red Sea
5   It's just possible he may be the hero. We are not sure yet. Have another look in case.
6   On the other hand, the hero may be Freddie Fane who dances divinely.
7   Now we can begin.
8   Lilian is very kindly taking her parents to a dance. It is the first dance she has taken them to for some time.
9   Freddie, of course, is going to the dance too.
10   There's no hurry. Freddie is coming for us in his car. (*Plus outline drawing of speeding sports car*)
11   Waiting for Freddie. (*Plus outline drawing of genie cocking a snook at Freddie from the exhaust fumes*)
12   "We are not amused". (*After Freddie arrives on his scooter, rather than with his car which has broken down*)
13   TaxEEE!
14   There is a room over there where you can play Bridge, father.
15   But your mother and I want to dance.
16   Come back in three hours. (*Freddie to blacked-up servant who brings them tea in mock-Oriental teahouse*)
17   This is the seventh time he has proposed to her this month. (*Plus outline of unfurling scroll calendar*)
18   If I ever marry it must be to a *man* who has done things. What have you ever done, Freddie?
19   I invented a new jazz the other day.
20   I ought to introduce myself. My name is John Brice.
21   Not the Great Explorer?
22   I've been reading *Through Trackless Paths*. It's wonderful how you find your way out of the jungle.
23   Do tell me some of your adventures.
24   John Brice discovers the Piebald Gorilla of Central Africa.
25   The Piebald Gorilla discovers John Brice.
26   No doubt a similar story was being told in Central Africa. (*Centre triangle of triptych, with Brice and Lilian in left triangle and male and female gorilla, right*)
27   He tells how he discovered the North Pole.
28   She's sitting out with a bicycle accident.
29   He tells how he discovered the Equator.
30   But however do you find your way?
31   JB's bump of locality compared with yours.

The publicity brochure for Minerva Films' comedy series declares that the company was attempting to get away from "the comic picture-postcard type of film which appropriates the trade name of comedy".[1] I take this to imply a shift away from the one-off slapstick joke of the seaside postcard towards a greater emphasis on story. Story is a key value in the British trade and review press, frequently cited as more important than stars.[2] British cinema, it is claimed, does not need stars because it has a rich fund of stories, already presold as popular literature. The "classics" of English literature *are* the stars, and hence adaptation requires a certain closeness to the original so that we may re-encounter old favourites.

However, "story" in the British trade press represents a different concept from the notion of "classic narrative" which, until recently, has dominated discussion of American cinema, with its emphasis on the seamless integration of elements into a coherent and transparently visualised story world, and equally seamless transition from one shot or episode to the next. In the practice of Minerva Films, "story" retains a number of features of the slapstick tradition – for example, direct address to the audience, the gag – but is transposed to a more literate level through the combination of intertitle and image. Hence the storytelling process – for example, *Bookworms* (1920) introduced as "A Comedy in Two Volumes" – is foregrounded by Minerva Films as a way of narrativising comedy and extending the boundaries of the picture postcard joke, rather than obliterating it.

Reliance on the pre-sold story and the literary-verbal skills of storytelling is frequently blamed for British filmmaking's lack of cinematic sense. But this means not a non-visual cinema, but rather a redefinition of the notion of the "cinematic". Indeed, we find story and picture peculiarly intertwined in British culture from the mid-19th and into the 20th centuries, including British genre painting, the Pre-Raphaelite marriage of poetic text and picture, and the rise of the illustrated press and vogue for book illustrations, in which picture and story often claim independent, if related, status.[3] Closer to the cinema, the widely popular magic lantern united narratives drawn from popular fictions and songs with illustrative images. Martin Meisel notes the retention by British painting of the literary, narrating caption long after the French moved towards "pure" paint, and, according to David Peters Corbett, this narrativising tendency persists into English modernism.[4] In the context of such widespread union of narrative and image, the literariness of British cinema is best understood not simply in reference to its source material, but to a "literateness" of the image – which gains autonomy as itself a "speaking", narrating image. This, in turn, provides a context for thinking about the relation of intertitles and image in silent British cinema, and in the Brunel/Milne collaborations in particular.

The first role of the titles in *The Bump* and *Bookworms* is to emphasise the shaping function of the storyteller – "Once Upon a Time" for *Bookworms*, "Now we can begin" in *The Bump*. But titles also ask us to participate in the role of an audience for a storytelling: "Better take another look at her as she's the heroine". In the first instance, therefore, this direct address, with its invitation to collude in the rituals and jokes of the storyteller, prevent images slipping past us in a continuous flow. Intertitles – as reviewers looking for American standards complain – interrupt the narrative illusion of a continuous world in order to *present* images as performing narrative elements. *The Bump* begins with the search for the hero. He "may be Freddie Fane who dances divinely", a title followed by the transliterating high-angle close-up on his Charlestoning feet which pulls out and up to focus on his ecstatic smile. Thus, two image elements are cut from a scene and, in conjunction with the positioning of the adverb "divinely", become articulate through the transference of literateness from title to image, retaining the gently ironic tone of the story*teller* and direct address to the audience. This effort to make the image literate, to produce a narrating image, leads, in Minerva Films, to the frequent integration of caption and image. "Waiting for Freddie" is combined with a line-drawing in which an evil genie, cocking a snook at Freddie, emerges out of the car exhaust, to be followed by the transliterating image of Lilian's mother wearily playing Patience. The witty intertitle exaggerates this process of transliteration by drawing attention to the hidden irony or comicality of the image to which – like "our errand boy" – it points: John Brice's facial scars explained by luggage labels.

The foregrounding of the storytelling process as an interaction between title and image permits the retention of heterogeneous and incongruous materials of the captioned picture postcard, turning images into signs and documents which we are required to read – we literally *read* John Brice's face. The process of producing a series of articulate, narrating and heterogeneous images, reinforced by use of iris, other masking frames and tableau effects, emphasises their boundedness, their discreteness, producing the discontinuities characteristic of British cinema. Thus, the dancing stops as Lilian and her family arrive at the fancy dress ball, posed across the front of the frame like a family photograph. As a result, images are made available as props for visual-verbal jokes through the possibility they offer for incongruous juxtapositions, following an absurdist or nonsensical logic which performs as a kind of literary slapstick. Freddie throws his arms out in a romantic gesture of proposal to be handed Lilian's empty teacup; the Great Explorer drops onto one knee to discover through his field-glasses the Piebald Gorilla, while, in the next shot, a pantomime animal, mimicking his gestures, discovers him. For all Minerva's ambition to uplift British film comedy, Brunel felt their venture justified when, thankfully, he heard the hearty laughter of the first trade show audience.[5]

Literary slapstick is in part to do with a play on literal meanings, and is connected, like the need for "literariness" itself, I want to suggest, to the insistently social nature of British culture. Its emphasis on articulation aims to identify story elements, plot situations, character types and narrative images in *class* terms in particular, but also in terms of gender, sexuality, ethnicity, nationality and – key to the Minerva comedies – generations. Having cut out the image, as it were, the wit lies in incongruous and satirical juxtapositions, which put different social elements at odds with each other. For example, Freddie buttoning his evening coat over his Eastern tunic, and John Brice transposing to the London streets the techniques of African exploration: "The author of *Through Trackless Paths* sights a Native Chief" – i.e. a man with a bowler hat and buttonhole. In this respect, the popular sources of British cinema – whether literary or pictorial – themselves represent social documents, defining different class, gender and generational attitudes; a new jazz vs. Bridge – but also reversing them: "But your mother and I want to dance".

It is not surprising that a literary cinema, founded on adaptation and the literary (or literal) document, is given to allusion and parody as a major source of comedy. Thus, the emphasis on storytelling both is self-referential and produces the core jokes in *Bookworms* and *The Bump*. *Bookworms* models itself on the fairy tale princess locked in her suburban castle, while Freddie nearly loses Lilian to her identification with the stories within the film story told to her – Chinese box-like – by the Great Explorer. In this context, I want to consider more closely the generational dimension to this storytelling comedy. The notion of storytelling as distinct from "classic" narration recalls the oral tradition which, in modern times, we encounter largely through childhood. And, of course, A A Milne is best-known today as the author of children's poetry and the stories of Winnie-the-Pooh (although, in his own time, he preferred to be known as a playwright). Indeed, the address of *The Bump* and *Bookworms* is that of the children's story. I turn here to Jackie Wullschläger who, in *Inventing Wonderland* (1995), situates Milne at the end of a 50-year tradition of writing for children which became a major narrative form from the mid-Victorian period to the end of the 1920s, including *Alice's Adventures in Wonderland* (1866), the nonsense verse of Edward Lear, *Peter Pan* (1904) and *The Wind in the Willows* (1908), and ending with the Pooh stories.[6] All these children's stories depend on a kind of nonsensical, absurdist fantasy and whimsical humour which is relevant not only to the Milne/Brunel collaborations, but also to much of British filmmaking of the period. Wullschläger suggests that these great children's stories arise out of the Victorian/Edwardian cult of childhood.

However, rather than idealising childhood, they use the perspective of the child, in his/her capacity to make anarchic connections while, at the same time, innocently taking the delusions and fantasies of adulthood at face value, to ironise and bring down their pretensions and hypocrisy, at the same time exposing the child in the adult. So, the Great Explorer, looking intently through binoculars for the Piebald Gorilla, does not notice the pantomime animal creeping up behind him. Lilian's literal identification exposes the exaggeration of his stories as she pulls a rug around her for the North Pole tale, or, conversely, fans herself when "He tells how he discovered the Equator"; later, he is reduced to childhood by a title which archly comments, as he sets out to find Stucoway Terrace: "He feels rather lonely. He has never been on an expedition by himself before."

However, Wullschläger's observations suggest links that reach beyond the parameters of children's literature. Many adult entertainments of this period partake in what might be seen as "child's play": from *tableaux vivants* at country-house parties to amateur theatricals and filmmaking, to the charades played, for example, by Novello and his friends into the small hours after playing in the theatre; to A A Milne's popular 1910 column for *Punch*, featuring The Rabbits – a twenty-something generation of "fast-talking hedonists who quip at each other across the croquet lawn and play eccentric games"[7] – a group to which Freddie and Lilian clearly belong. *Bookworms*, constructed as a whimsical parody of the fairy tale, explicitly invokes its audience as children:

Title: Whom has he seen?
T: We'll give you three guesses.
T: 1?
T: 2?
T: No, your last chance.
T: She ...

In the same vein, alongside Alice's "Wonderland", J M Barrie's "Never Never Land" and Milne's "Hundred Acre Wood at the Top of the Forest", we find newspaper and magazine columns headed "Notes from Theatreland" or "Filmland". A key feature of such child's play is dressing up and role-play, with the possibility of disguise and role change. It is no accident that Lilian and Freddie met the Great Explorer at a fancy dress ball – nor, as the title "Freddie, of course, is going to the dance too" hints, that it is Freddie, rather than Lilian, who plays the Cinderella of the piece, searching the fancy dress shop for a suitable Eastern tunic to wear to the ball, while Lilian goes as herself.

If British cinema as a literary and literal cinema is about socially locating and defining its dramatis personae for the recognition of a class-, gendered-, ethnic- and generation-bound society, regression into the arena of child's play offers a space where roles can be swapped, and boundaries and identities thrown into experimental confusion. Amateur theatre or filmmaking was, for some, a means of escape from the constrictions and conventions of their class. Brian Aherne's mother, for example, was prohibited from going on the stage, but found outlet in amateur theatricals, sometimes making guest appearances at the Birmingham Playhouse. Lady Diana Manners made a much-publicised appearance in the first Prizma Colour film, *The Glorious Adventure* (1922), which dramatised the Fire of London, while Brunel himself appeared in amateur theatre in Brighton. Milne and others of the intelligentsia drawn to cinema, such as Brunel, Ivor Montagu and Anthony Asquith, were all acutely aware of the constrictions of their class position, and saw in cinema, as opposed to the traditional arts, a means of negotiating the highbrow/ lowbrow distinction which emerged in English cultural consciousness at the turn of the century. In this context, the literariness that taps into child's play calls up pantomime and fairy tale for their possibilities of class, gender, ethnic and generational transformations. Such transformations are much-needed by a society in which an evolving social democracy demands closer social class interaction; for which postwar paternalist authority is at issue; for which the question "What do women want?" presses; and for which Britain's imperial mission is beginning to show strains. In such a context, *The Bump* invites us to submit self-consciously to the playful teasing of the storyteller, who manipulates acculturated and speaking images to produce ironic and parodic juxtapositions and reversals which bring down the pretensions of generational, class, gendered and imperial authority by mixing the dignified with the low. Thus, the panto Piebald Gorilla mocks the imperial adventurer, as does the game played by the blacked-up band, jazzing wildly behind John Brice's back and falling into mock-obedient silence every time he turns his steely patriarchal stare in their direction. Similarly, "Boys' Own" colonial presumptions are challenged not simply by the absurdity of the panto gorilla, but by the formula of reverse discovery as the animal looks back.

I would like to conclude with a final reference to Jackie Wullschläger, who argues that Milne marks a shift from his predecessors in his greater realism about the nature of the child, who is not allowed dominance but is subject to a two-way irony in which the child's presumptions are also cut down to size. Thus, Lilian, positioned in an early scene at the apex of the shot as an ironising onlooker at her parents practising dance steps, is put in her place by an intertitle which quips, "Lilian is very kindly taking her parents to a dance. It is the first dance she has taken them to for some time." For Wullschläger, the Winnie-the-Pooh stories represent a taming of "Wonderland" in which the toys (not "real" animals) are themselves the subject of mockery. However, I would like to approach the Milne/Brunel collaborations and Brunel's later work which moves towards a more aggressively hysterical form of burlesque from a different perspective. In Filmland – as a place of regression to child's play with all the forms the culture throws up – there is no place secure from irony, parody and mockery. In the Minerva productions, child and adult meet on the same terrain on almost equal terms: in Brunel's later films, they become one. *Battling Bruisers* (1925), for example, has Brunel playing multiple roles, including the match compère – the Rt Hon Lord Pifford, the famous sporting peer – and visiting Prince Olarf of Yugo-Slowa in a boxing burlesque played out in different parodic national styles from England, Paris and Spain to revolutionary Russia, concluding with Lenin calling the shots in Hyde Park in a satirical montage style that anticipates the extremes of Dziga Vertov's *Chelovek s kinoapparatom (Man With a Movie Camera*, 1929). Unlike the great Victorian and Edwardian writers who, unable to unravel the problematics of their age, clung to the creative possibilities of a perspective rooted in childhood, Brunel's recourse to child's play, deracinated from the certainties of the past age and unable to commit to those which are galvanising Europe, turns on the liberal scepticism of the innocent eye. Perhaps the best that can be achieved in a class-bound society bent on liberal reform, rather than revolution, is this recourse to child's play, whereby all social positions can, through the fantasy of Filmland and the doubleness of parody, be kept *in play*.

Notes

[1]   Minerva Films publicity brochure, British Film Institute Special Collections.

[2]   See, for example, Maurice Elvey, "Why There Are No British Male Stars", *Stoll's Editorial News* 3: 12 (5 August 1920): 7-8.

[3]   See Michael R Booth, *Victorian Spectacular Theatre: 1850-1910* (Boston; London; Henley: Routledge & Kegan Paul, 1981), and Martin Meisel, *Realizations: Narrative, Pictorial, and Theatrical Arts in Nineteenth-Century England* (Princeton, NJ: Princeton University Press, 1983).

[4]   David Peters Corbett, *The modernity of English art: 1914-30* (Manchester; New York: Manchester University Press, 1997).

[5]   Adrian Brunel, *Nice Work: The Story of Thirty Years in British Film Production* (London: Forbes Robertson, 1949): 61.

[6]   Jackie Wullschläger, *Inventing Wonderland: The Lives and Fantasies of Lewis Carroll, Edward Lear, J. M. Barrie, Kenneth Grahame and A. A. Milne* (London: Methuen, 1995).

[7]   Ibid: 181.

Parody on the Fringes: Adrian Brunel, Minority Film Culture and the Art of Deconstruction

Jamie Sexton

A small number of parody films, or comic experiments, existed on the fringes of the British film industry in the latter half of the 1920s. These films need to be seen in the context of minority film culture of the period, with which many of the filmmakers involved had links. For example, Adrian Brunel and Ivor Montagu, both of whom made parodic comedies, were founding members of the Film Society, the first exhibition outlet in Britain exclusively devoted to screening films that lay outside the mainstream circuit. Attention will centre on the figure of Adrian Brunel, especially his burlesque of expedition films, *Crossing the Great Sagrada* (1924). But I will also briefly consider his other burlesque films, in addition to other related films, such as those which Montagu made in association with Frank Wells, and *C.O.D. – A Mellow Drama* (1929), a parody of German Expressionism. In contrast with the relative neglect that such films have suffered in general film histories, these films will be related to discourses both of the time and of more recent origin in an attempt to get to grips with some of the meanings to which they give rise. It will emerge that these films can be read as deconstructive critiques of certain elements that characterised film culture, elements that were perceived as restrictive and formulaic. By contrast, the playfulness and mocking humour that characterise these films constitute a curiously postmodern aesthetic that exposes pomposity, stringent rules and false authenticity. This counters the widely adopted assumption that alternative British film culture in this period was merely pompous and élitist.

It is useful firstly to explore some of the aspects of alternative British film culture that can be linked to the themes and methods of these fringe comedy films. "Alternative British film culture" refers to those activities of the period that challenged some of the elements of mainstream film culture, especially the more conservative elements. These two cultures were not totally opposed; on the contrary, some elements of the cultures overlapped, and this is evident in the activities of certain personnel, such as Brunel and Montagu, who were active in both spheres. Many artists involved in alternative British film culture of this time were not opposed to mainstream culture *per se*, but wanted to alter it for the better, and thus often intervened in it. Crudely speaking, these two cultures can be set out as follows:

• ALTERNATIVE	MAINSTREAM
• Film as art	Film as entertainment/commerce
• Independence, eclecticism, experiment	Restrictions and rules
• Anti-censorship	Pro-censorship
• Anti-theatrical	Theatrical

- International   Nationalist
- Highbrow   Lowbrow and middlebrow

This oppositional dichotomy should not be seen as strict and fixed, but as a representation of extremes: aesthetes would in general veer towards the alternative, and the commercially-minded towards the mainstream, but there would also be exceptions and overlaps. For example, mainstream films would sometimes place importance upon artistry; overall, however, alternative film culture emphasised this theme more consistently.

The Film Society and the journal *Close Up* (the first British film journal to cover the artistic side of film as its main emphasis) are the most famous and lasting representatives of alternative British film culture in the late-1920s. They are both symptoms of a growing fissure in British film culture which led to the formulation of many ideas and practices diverging from what had previously characterised British film culture.

For the most part, the dominant commercial cinema regarded the alternative film culture with suspicion; it saw it not only as a threat and a critique, but also as over-serious, pompous, snobbish and even "freakish".[1] Certainly, not all of this criticism was unjust: *Close Up* did often display a prejudicial snobbism towards mainstream film culture that is worthy of reproach. However, many of these criticisms were overstated, and, if the alternative culture is analysed, one evident feature is a tendency to satirise and debunk. This tendency stems from a desire to evade over-formulaic approaches to filmmaking, and to resist being "straitjacketed" into a coherent function. It was not only "mainstream" British film culture that was the victim of satire and mockery; aspects of art cinema and avant-garde filmmaking were also mocked, especially those perceived as pretentious. Even in the pages of *Close Up* (the most pompous alternative force) we can find articles that criticise formulaic pretension in certain avant-garde movements, as well as in Hollywood cinema. Oswell Blakeston, for instance, wrote many satirical articles mocking the Parisian avant-garde, and also made a film on the same topic, *I Do Like To Be Beside the Seaside* (1927).[2] Likewise, Kenneth Macpherson excoriated the French specialist film circles as being too caught up in fashionable trends, and guilty of "mental kowtowing".[3]

Such sceptical tendencies led to those such as Brunel being hyper-aware of particular filmic codes and conventions. When such codes and conventions could be seen as negative, restrictive or "naturalised", it was inevitable that people would eventually denaturalise them by messing around with them in a playful and self-conscious manner. Such an attitude grew partly out of the *eclecticism* of alternative British film culture during this period. Because this culture arose not out of a set of production activities, but instead out of a primary aim to transform the scope and quality of films that were exhibited, there was an openness within this culture to view as many types of films as possible. The Film Society, for instance, showed a vast array of different films, including German Expressionism, abstract animation, Soviet montage, scientific studies, sport films, comedies, resurrections of old shorts, and many more. It can be seen as not only the first alternative British exhibition site, but also the first film school in Britain, whereby a vast array of codes and styles could be studied. In fact, the Film Society even stated that one of its aims was "to encourage the study of cinematography"; it also arranged lectures and discussions "on the art and technique of film".[4] It is precisely this eclectic feature and the culture's primary reliance upon consumption, rather than production, that have led many theorists to dismiss British alternative activities as parasitic and derivative. In order to privilege the "genius" creator, this view ignores the way in which all creation is an assemblage of pre-existing components;

it also reveals an inadequate framework within which to understand such activities.[5]

If it is accepted that all creation is, at least to some extent, re-creation, questions of innovation must be recast. Originality ceases to become a transcendent invention of new methods, but instead becomes a way of approaching and arranging so that it appears distinctive and sheds new light on pre-existing components.[6]

If we take Brunel as an example, we could say that his "burlesque" films are parasitic in that they depend upon other forms in order to mock them. They do not even intend to innovate, but are merely content to mimic what has gone before. On the other hand, it can be argued that these films innovate through the unique aesthetic that they initiate. Brunel's burlesque films, in their extreme self-consciousness, in the manner in which they foreground filmic conventions, and through the way in which they cut and paste a range of multi-media materials, predate postmodernism and deconstruction. Brunel is thus an innovator through the way in which he puts a new spin upon what is already happening. Whereas many modernist experiments camouflaged their parasitic traces in order to promote their "originality", Brunel exposes such traces, and, in the process, calls into question existing notions of originality.[7] It may be that such an aesthetic was encouraged through the limited finances that Brunel had at his disposal, but this does not immediately invalidate such claims: many others who worked with limited finances did not forge identical aesthetic paths.

Brunel produced a number of burlesque films which arose out of his precarious plight as a director of mainstream films. After directing his first commercial feature film *The Man Without Desire* (1923), he was temporarily unable to get any directorial work in the commercial film industry until the making of *Blighty* (1927). This gave him the incentive to undertake some personal projects or, as he called them, "experiments in ultra-cheap cinematography".[8] He had previously worked within the realm of short comedies in his collaborations with A A Milne for the company Minerva Films (which he helped to set up). The difference between these films and his burlesques was that, in the latter, Brunel took creative charge (he was producer and financier for his first two films), and this led him to adopt a more anarchic and less restrained style. His first burlesque, *Crossing the Great Sagrada*, was a spoof of the "expedition" film, mocking the title of Angus Buchman's film, *Crossing the Great Sahara* (1924). According to Brunel, the film cost £80 and was composed of a third of titles, a third of footage from old travel pictures, and a third of himself dressed in various costumes.[9] Brunel made another burlesque in the same year, *Pathetic Gazette*, a satire of the newsreel film, made for £90. In 1925, he made five further burlesques for Michael Balcon and C M Woolf at Gainsborough Pictures: *Battling Bruisers* (a parody of the boxing film), *The Blunderland of Big Game* (of the wildlife film), *So This Is Jollygood* (filmmaking), *Cut It Out* (censorship) and *A Typical Budget* (another newsreel satire).[10]

In *Crossing the Great Sagrada*, Brunel utilises various elements (found footage, parodic film, titles, animation) in order to create a collage-type film that satirises many of the conventions that make up the film world. In particular, Brunel is attacking the explosion of "expedition" films, especially the manner in which many of them were merely exploiting codified formulae in predictable ways, and also the nationalist and imperialist boasting that informed them.

Anti-nationalist traits were a key feature of alternative British film culture. Most of the people involved in this culture believed that film art was an international phenomenon, and that it should not in any way be hindered by nationalist restrictions. The plans to create specifically British films in an effort to boost imperial strength were anathema to alternative aesthetes, who craved the chance to promote films from around the world. *Crossing the Great Sagrada* combines this theme with anti-illusionist satire in order to denaturalise the codes through which celluloid heroism is established. The first title, for example, proclaims in capitals: "An All British Production". If there is any doubt about the satirical nature of this, one should note that throughout the film the titles are always punning (for example, "an indolent film", "a thirst national attraction"), or creating a comic disjuncture with the image (such as when the titles indicate that the scene is set in Wapping, and the following picture shows a small village of mud-huts). The racism of such imperialist narratives is also mocked through the comic exaggeration of the fetishistic attention paid to the "differences" in dress and ritual, such as the shot of the villager with an excessively large nosering.

On one level, the film can be seen not as a self-reflexive exercise in drawing attention to film codes, but as a critique of "fake" naturalism (as opposed to "authenticity"). Support for such a reading is provided by the fact that, at the time, some of the expedition films caused outrage because they faked scenes. Rachael Low has written how Richard Kearton "reconstructed" episodes of travellers in the sand wastes of the Sahara in his 1924 film *Toto's Wife*.[11] In this sense, Brunel's film is a satire of the way in which such films are pretending to be something that they are not, rather than a self-reflexive analysis of cinematic codes *per se*. The drawing of attention to the fact that the desert scenes are shot on Blackpool beach, and the other references to scenes which are "faked", such as the obvious animation of camels, back this up. Exaggeratedly chaotic aspects of the film, such as illogical jumps and a generally messy image-narrative overtly papered over by titles, can also be seen in this light. They can be read as a critique of the way in which many expedition films were exploitative constructions coherently pieced together by editing, rather than authentic representations.

Although such satire does not, in itself, constitute any radically subversive activity (its comic elements are its main emphasis), I would argue that there are reasons to claim that it is more than just an attack upon inauthenticity. Firstly, the film itself continually revels in the exposing of filmic construction: for instance, the scenes at the beginning which show Brunel and his assistant Lionel Rich as themselves, followed by a comic fiction portraying the financier of the film and his staff, are not specific attacks upon expedition films, but are a satire of filmmaking in general (revealing the boasting of promotion and the necessity of funding). Secondly, as I have already noted, Brunel attacked a wide variety of different elements in his other burlesques. Thirdly, the fact that Brunel worked in a wide variety of milieus and genres (propaganda films, light-hearted comedies, shadowplays, burlesques, scripts for cartoons, feature film direction), and that he was a member of the Film Society meant that he was well-versed in different codes and conventions for different types of films. This would have increased his sensitivity towards the way in which arbitrary codes could become established as "naturalised" modes of expression. And it was one of the aims of the alternative film culture of the day to counter the restrictions upon filmmaking practices, and to encourage more freedom. In this sense, the burlesque films can be seen as a continual attack upon any filmic codes that turn into restrictive and proscriptive rules. They are less an attack on that which is not authentic than an attack on film codes and styles that have become *falsely equated* with authenticity.[12]

This is the sense in which Brunel – in his burlesque films – operates as a debunker of master codes and narratives, especially those seen as in some way oppressive. This is why the subjects of attack are themes such as stereotypes, imperialism, censorship and nationalism. This is why they have an air of anarchic joy about them, for they are delighting in the playful deconstruction of authoritative elements. His style evinces many traits that have been identified with postmodernism and deconstructionism: he offers no blueprint for future creativity in these films; rather, he simply critiques existing styles in a way that nevertheless constitutes a distinctive aesthetic. He not only revels in mocking authority/the master code, but also, in the process, uncovers the transparency of representational codes. He does this by utilising existing footage, mixing this with parodic titles, and, in the process, transforming signifying systems through contextual shuffling. (For example, using the same footage and transforming its meaning by placing it in a completely different context to that in which it originally appeared.) It is through this methodology that Brunel constructs an accessible range of films in which attention is drawn to the fabricated nature of filmmaking. As his subjects are usually film types that he sees as formulaic or stereotypical, he thus offers a critique of constricting ways of making films, and thus encourages others to escape such restrictions (all the while having fun doing so).

Several other films were made around the fringes of the British film industry in the late-1920s, and can be linked to the alternative British film culture of the period. Like Brunel's films, they create a distinct aesthetic through the way in which they parody or deconstruct codes. For example, Ivor Montagu – who ran an editing company with Brunel and who was Chairman of the Film Society – made three films with Frank Wells, his father, H G Wells, and Elsa Lanchester. These films can be seen as milder versions of the same theme (deconstructive mockery). Although films such as *Bluebottles* and *Daydreams* (both 1928) are more coherent in their narrative structure and less overtly parodic, *Bluebottles* manages to mock the authority of the police, while *Daydreams* deconstructs Hollywood-type glamour, revealing it to be nothing more than surface embellishment. Another film, *C.O.D. – A Mellow Drama*, privately made in 1929 by technicians at the Stoll studios during the transition to sound, utilises the codes of German Expressionism. The film plays upon "recognisable" codes, such as lots of dark shadows and a mysterious narrative, and compresses them into an approximate time span of eleven minutes. In compressing and parodying the codes familiar to German Expressionism, the film creates its own unique aesthetic: a kind of fragmented, elliptical mystery in which the narrative signs become overdetermined and thus foregrounded. Self-reflexive aesthetics also pop up in mainstream feature films such as Anthony Asquith's *Shooting Stars* (1928). This feature, although less chaotic and fragmented, has similarities with the Brunel burlesques such as *So This Is Jollygood*. Asquith was also a member of the Film Society.

It is possible that the eclectic nature of alternative British film culture led it to distrust the adoption of any deeply committed stance, thus influencing its humorous currents (which can be seen as a defence against pomposity). Even those artists who have been identified with avant-gardism (due mainly to the manner in which their abstraction fits into a modernist framework), such as Len Lye and Norman McLaren, often evinced a light-hearted playfulness in their work. This distrust of pomposity and formula is thus linked to the manner in which a vast array of different styles were seen by such people. This led them to shift between styles, seeing a style as only one permutation amongst many, and therefore not overestimating the importance of one at the expense of another. It also encouraged them to critique a style when it was seen to have congealed into a hackneyed formula. Brunel, who worked in many different genres, production milieus and capacities (director, producer, editor, scriptwriter, actor), could be seen as the most representative member of such eclectic mutability. One of the reasons why this eclecticism and mutability was valuable was that it helped increase one's chances of gaining employment in the unpredictable world of British filmmaking. A second reason, however, reinforced by the subjects of his films, is that it helped to evade being pinned down and restricted. It is possibly the difficulty in pinning down many of the characters involved within such a culture that has led to their neglect; such schizophrenia is hard to accommodate within conventional critical and historiographical frameworks of British cinema.

Notes

[1]   The trade press largely perceived the Film Society as a threat and a criticism of its own activities. In reaction to the Film Society, it labelled the "alternative" culture as a fringe collection of misfits, interested in "failures". For instance, in an editorial regarding the Society, *The Bioscope* criticised it along such lines. It argued: "With a few exceptions, this curiously assorted programme can only be designated as a collection of freak films which certainly does not represent the film industry in any respect. And it seems fairly certain that the only films that the Society will be able to secure for exclusive presentation are similar freaks and throw-outs. A 'critical tradition' can hardly be established by an intensive study of the film producer's failures, however brilliant those failures, in some cases, may have been." ("Things that Matter", *The Bioscope* 64: 989 [24 September 1925]: 38.) Brunel himself had to forgo his place on the Film Society Council Board due to the concern of his employees, Gainsborough. He writes: "I had long ceased to be a member of the Council, as my employers insisted that my association with the Society would damage the prestige of the films that I made for them!". See Adrian Brunel, *Nice Work: The Story of Thirty Years in British Film Production* (London: Forbes Robertson, 1949): 114.

[2]   This film appears to be lost. It starred, amongst others, the poet H.D., and was described at the time as a spoof on French, as well as German and Russian avant-garde techniques. See *The Architectural Review* 67 (1930): 341.

[3]   See, especially, Kenneth Macpherson, "As Is", *Close Up* 6: 1 (January 1930): 2. In this article, he accuses the avant-garde Parisian film culture of "movieosophy", described as "a process of mental kowtowing indulged in by dreamy bores". Blakeston even wrote an "alternative" book on filmmaking, which was a parody of prescriptive film manuals that nevertheless lapsed into prescribing its own values: see Oswell Blakeston, *Through a Yellow Glass* (London: Pool, 1928).

[4]   *The Film Society Special Collection, item 2: Constitution and Rules of the Film Society Limited* (British Film Institute Library, Special Collections).

[5]   The theory that creation is an assemblage of pre-existing components is philosophically propounded within the various works of Gilles Deleuze and Félix Guattari. For instance, they state that "invention is a conjugation or connection of different flows". See Gilles Deleuze and Félix Guattari, *A Thousand Plateaus: Capitalism and Schizophrenia*, translated by Brian Massumi (London: The Athlone Press, 1988): 219. Creation, for them, is the combination of flows that open up new pathways, as opposed to the propagation of pathways already crossed.

[6]   Rosalind E Krauss argues that the one thing that holds constant in modernist-vanguardist discourses is the theme of originality, of the artist constructing something new, free from tradition. She argues that this is a fiction because it bases itself upon the assumption that there is "an indisputable zero-ground beyond which there is no further model, or referent, or text". See Rosalind E Krauss, *The Originality of the Avant-Garde and Other Modernist Myths* (London; Cambridge, MA: The MIT Press, 1986): 160. By contrast, she argues that all that modernist works succeed in doing is "locating the signifier of another, prior system of grids, which have beyond them, yet another, even earlier system". Ibid: 162.

[7]   Krauss argues that modernist/avant-garde artists utilised techniques of both reproduction and uniqueness, multiplicity and singularity, yet "repressed" the reproductive signifiers in order to promote those that referred to uniqueness.

[8]   Adrian Brunel, "Experiments in Ultra-Cheap Cinematography", *Close Up* 3: 4 (October 1928): 43-46.

[9]   Ibid: 44.

[10]   Ibid. He also completed a private burlesque for C M Woolf made for the first anniversary of the Shepherd's Bush Pavilion. This film was entitled *Money for Nothing*; made for £65, it was about the "cut-throat methods of the film trade" (ibid: 45). He also

made a private film with Ivor Montagu entitled *Love, Life and Laughter* (1923). In addition he made a very short film entitled *Brunel and Montagu* in 1928, a private movie made by the editing company of the same name.

[11]   Rachael Low, *The History of the British Film 1918-1929* (London: George Allen & Unwin, 1971): 288.

[12]   The difference is that Brunel is not claiming any filmic authenticity. Through his continual exposing of codes and conventions, he is drawing attention to the fact that all film is a construction. He attacks those conventions that are anathema to his vision.

Funny Peculiar and Funny Ha-Ha:
Some Preliminary Observations on Men in
Frocks in Early British Cinema

Amy Sargeant

George Meredith's "Essay on Comedy", republished in 1897, echoes Polonius' announcement of the players in *Hamlet* in the distinction it draws between different theatrical genres, and in its identification of various composite forms. Meredith provides a taxonomy of the comic in literature and drama, and maps types of comedy of which national characteristics are idiosyncratically accommodating. He condemns the English "so-called Comedy of Manners" as vacuous, but praises English prose and poetry as often delightful, delicate and graceful. "Generally, however," he says, "the English elect excel in satire, and they are noble humorists. The national disposition is for hard-hitting, with a moral purpose to sanction it; or for rosy, sometimes larmoyant, geniality...and with a singular attraction for thick-headedness, to decorate it with asses' ears and the most beautiful sylvan haloes".[1] Meredith endorses a familiar Continental observation that English humour draws on a store of bile and tends towards the splenetic.

This essay aims to discuss the variety of humour which cross-dressing serves in early British – or rather, English – cinema in the period before the First World War. It is apparent that men in frocks are not necessarily humorous (indeed, it was far from the intention of some stage cross-dressers to serve Meredith's brand of "thick-headed" humour), that different types of drag can be undertaken and perceived either seriously or frivolously, but that drag has more chance of raising a laugh when employed in certain performances and in certain situations. The androgynous ambiguity of The Splinters concert party, formed by ex-servicemen in 1918, possibly elicits less of a laugh when it performs its act (a genial camp precursor of Matthew Bourne's *Swan Lake* [1997/1999]), and was more intent to amuse when the men were reassuringly seen as men, joking raucously, legs akimbo, backstage after the show. "Proof that men are deceivers ever!", reads the Pathé intertitle, addressing the review's presumed female audience. Furthermore, there are particular characters who are, or were, found funny whether performed by men or by women. I am concerned with three issues here: firstly, to consider how cross-dressing was used; secondly, to identify characters and situations which are the butt of jokes, but which may or may not be cross-dressed; and thirdly, to suggest where these characters and situations come from, in substance and in kind, in terms of stage and other precedents, and to consider, gesturally, where they went to.

It is possible to sort the material schematically, according to these considerations, but experience indicates that there were also circumstantial and expedient reasons for using men in female roles. In early comedies and facials – the simple, often single-shot films which concentrated on the grimaces and facial contortions of the performers – verisimilitude was often quite beside the point, and types (especially in menial comic roles) were presented as types. Sometimes one recognises recurrent figures, and one suspects that men are playing women simply because they are available as part of a stock company. Focused historic research might serve to establish exactly what personnel were at hand. One could speculate that it might have been thought an unsuitable or impossible job for an elderly lady to perform some of the antics of her comic surrogates. Sometimes dressing as a woman may render a gag more vulgarly comic. I am simply not sure as yet, but it does seem worth making this qualification clear at the outset, and I do acknowledge Luke McKernan's advice[2] not to build over-elaborate theses to explain (or, worse, to explain away) some apparently quite simple and perhaps self-evident material.

Cross-dressing in cinema has obvious antecedents in particular music-hall and variety turns, and in dame roles in pantomime. Jackie Bratton has discussed a number of Edwardian travesty performers and concludes that the English music-hall was "notoriously misogynistic".[3] Certainly, individuals and groups which sought to advance the political and social rights of women were not generally well-received. Songs lampooned those who would turn the world topsy-turvy, "men in skirts and women in trousers", and sketches presented a caricature "Mrs Spankfirst": such is the thrust of Paul's *The Lady Barber* (1898), the Riley Brothers' *Women's Rights* (1900) and Cricks and Martin's *Finding Your Counterpart* (1913). Emasculating lady barbers reappear in Clarendon's 1915 *Timothy Toddles*, at a training college for ladies, "to enable them to fill posts formerly held by men". In *Milling the Militants* (also Clarendon, 1913), the harridan Mrs Brown dumps the children on her husband in order to demonstrate with her suffragette sisters. In his dreams, Mr Brown becomes Prime Minister, is visited by David Lloyd George, and legislates for the suppression of the suffragettes: a fitting punishment for setting fire to pillar boxes is to shame women into six weeks in trousers... They apparently do not take to men's work and menswear after all. In Pinero's play *The Weaker Sex* (1888), Mrs Boyle-Chewton, leader of the Union of Independent Women, wears a costume which is severe, dowdy and ungainly, with her hair cut straight and short. "Why can't women vote?", she demands of Lord Gillingham. "They can", he retorts. "They tell the man how to". The suffragettes responded in kind to these frequent attacks in the halls and on the legitimate stage with similar mocking humour. For example, the eponymous hero of Gertrude Colmore's story "George Lloyd", published in the weekly woman's suffrage newspaper, is a suffragette in disguise. Depictions of suffragettes and other modern women are often "masculinised" in dress, manner and performance but are not necessarily enacted by men. Sportswomen, as in *Wife: The Weaker Vessel* (1915), and academics are also jibed at, sometimes for ineptitude in the activity itself (women should not attempt what men do better), and sometimes, by extension, in the assumption that they must thereby somehow be, or become, less femininely attractive (men do not make passes at girls who wear glasses or cycling gear).

The most obvious transferrals from stage to screen of drag roles would seem to be the filmed performances of star dames: for example, Warwick Trading Company's recordings of the Drury Lane performances by Dan Leno in his famous characterisation of Sister Anne. Leno's stage personae also included skivvy types of the "Widow Twankey" and "Old Mother Riley" variety. The revue stage included spoofs of "higher-class" theatrical pieces which sometimes employed cross-dressing, as in the enormously successful melodrama *The Colleen Bawn* (1860), and also mimicked figures familiar in magazines and advertising, such as "The Gibson Girl". George Robey's stage performance as the original for Pears' Baby, from John Everett Millais' "Bubbles" (1886), is some sort of a precedent for the *Did'ums* series; more immediately, however, it satirises by exaggeration the fashion of dressing and grooming infant girls and boys alike as if they were would-be angels. Did'ums wreaks havoc, and embarrasses and thwarts the plans of his elders and betters – as in *Daddy's Little Did'ums Did It* (1910), when he stows away to Paris in an oversized hatbox and then climbs into the nuptial bed.

The frustration of amorous intentions is itself another common subject. Sometimes the spoilsport is the butt of the joke, or at other times an individual for whom any such encounter is presupposed preposterous. Although often a woman, and often middle-aged or elderly, this is not always the case: in Gaumont's *The Tramp's Surprise* (1902), a man dresses himself as his girlfriend and shocks a flirtatious tramp. G A Smith's *The Old Maid's Valentine* (1900) tells a tale of hopes at first raised, then disappointed, and dignity affronted, while in the same director's *The Other Side of the Hedge* (1905) it is the matronly chaperone at whose expense we laugh. In the later *Love and the Varsity* (1913), the headmistress of the local finishing school, Miss Spinster, is ridiculed first for failing to recognise the Varsity boys in disguise, and then for failing to prevent the elopement: with axe in hand, she arrives at the Registry Office just in time to see them wed.

The tradition of segregated schools and colleges provides the subject-matter of much situation comedy. For Pinero, single-sex institutions (academic and religious) are the occasion for jokes about impropriety and inappropriate or incongruous behaviour: *The Schoolmistress* (1886) leads a double life as an operetta diva; men are found in the house after hours (as in Hepworth's *Tilly's Party* [1911]), and one girl has married secretly without parental consent. In *Dandy Dick* (1887), a tweedy matriarch cajoles men of the cloth into the sport of kings. Max Beerbohm has stone emperors perspiring at the very sight of Zuleika Dobson. "Mainly architectural, the beauties of Oxford", he remarks:

> True, the place is no longer one-sexed. There are the virguncules
> of Somerville and Lady Margaret's Hall; but beauty and the lust
> for learning have yet to be allied. There are the innumerable wives
> and daughters around the Parks, running in and out of their little
> red-brick villas; but the indignant shade of celibacy seems to have
> called down on the dons a Nemesis which precludes them from
> either marrying beauty or begetting it.[4]

A key archetype was *Charley's Aunt* (1892), a role written for W S Penley and first performed by him in 1892. With bow-window hair, bonnet and lace fichu, it is a familiar figure, from Lady Agatha d'Ascoyne (in *Kind Hearts and Coronets* [1949]), to *The Daily Express* Giles cartoon "Grandma". Brandon Thomas has one student dressing as another's Brazilian aunt (where the nuts come from, he says) in order to provide a suitable companion for two young ladies to whom his chums intend to propose, while Percy Stow's *Love and the Varsity* has two students dressing as girls as a means of effecting an entrance to the Ladies' Seminary. Both *Charley's Aunt* and *Love and the Varsity* rely for some of their humour on the disjuncture between "male" mannerisms and "female" garb, as when the chaps in *Love and the Varsity* perform riotously modern dances. Seemingly, their girlfriends and colleagues do not at first see through the disguise, and the boys are welcomed simply as girls who want to have more fun than is allowed, and, of course, Miss Spinster is keen to stop them. Situational cross-dressing comedies often employ character types which are masculinised in anticipation of their being asexual or desexualised. From *Love and the Varsity* to *Old Mother Riley, Headmistress* (1945), from the *St. Trinian's* series (1954-80) to *Nuns on the Run* (1990), part of the humour derives from the non-recognition by other characters of patently cross-dressed men as male.

Dick's *The Actor's Handbook and Guide to the Stage* (1884) gives the following advice to aspirant amateurs:

> The coquettish affectation of a young lady is displayed by many
> unnatural gestures and continual admiration of her own sweet
> self...That of the old maid is displayed by an awkward imitation of
> youth and juvenile manners...The affectation of fashion in an old
> maid is expressed by pompousness of accent, combined with
> extreme awkwardness...Such characters can seldom be overacted.[5]

The comedy of cross-dressing often lies in gross and grotesque exaggeration. While women are derided for being supposedly negligent of their appearance or for having allowed themselves to grow conspicuously older, jokes may still, conversely, be made at their expense for undue vanity. In 1905, George Grossmith (of *Diary of a Nobody* [1892] fame) ran a revue with Henry Gratton, in which the latter performed in drag in a chorus line with two women, and in which he played alternately "flapper" and "skivvy" types.

The mysteries and machinations of the woman's toilet, the masquerading process, as it were, the travesty which women routinely perpetrate, often figure in film. These are statements about women, rather than studied replications. In *Boudoir Secrets* (1902), the removal of the mask extends to the hair and teeth. In *Lord Algy's Beauty Show* (1908), women's dress is literally aped and ridiculed. In Gaumont's *How Percy Won the Beauty Competition* (1909), the camera pans across the line of smiling belles; one flirts outrageously and takes a tipple from a flask. Here again, the ruse is not noticed until the prize is awarded and Percy's two sidekicks reveal the disguise.

Theoretical approaches to comedy seem to be largely unwieldy, unyielding and dissatisfying, if only because of their stultifying effect on their subject-matter. Structuralists have tended to focus on the mechanisms of a joke or gag, its pattern of congruence, repetition, false trails and disjuncture. This throws little light on the reception or function of comedy in a particular context, or on particular comedians. Freud discusses joke-work as if it accorded with some third law of thermodynamics, but does offer possible subjective and social explanations as to why laughter occurs: "[t]he main characteristic of joke-work [is] liberating pleasure by getting rid of inhibitions".[6] His analysis is useful inasmuch as it draws attention to a cultural context, to the subjects considered permissible as the butt of a joke, and to the sorts of shorthand (in Freudian terms, condensation) employed in words, gestures and appearance. Henri Bergson interprets humour organically, but again draws attention to the function of different varieties of comedy in particular circumstances. Its means, he says, include repetition, inversion and reciprocal inversion, including exaggeration and degradation: "However spontaneous it seems, laughter always implies a kind of secret free-masonry, or even complicity with other laughers, real or imaginary". It depends, he argues, on social prejudice. Laughter for Bergson is a corrective gesture, even (one might conclude) a normalising one.[7]

On the other hand, it is no more than a commonplace to recognise in both cross-dressing and comedy (especially satire) the potential for the subversion of social and cultural norms. But this is not the immediate effect of the films which I have been describing here. There is, if anything, a more "corrective" exercise in play. Certainly, the films viewed so far bring to mind the rumbustious antics, questionable humour and "worst possible taste" of venture scouts and junior medics, rather than glamorous and/or ambiguous transvestism. There may be something of Lily Savage here, but not a lot of Eddie Izzard. Early comedy – after all, the mainstay of early cinema – presents itself in this regard as thoroughly mainstream. It uses simple, often violent, gags and visual humour which relies upon the ready recognition of character and situation. However, it does seem that in British comedy some of these character types and situations have been peculiarly long-lasting.

Notes

1   George Meredith, *An Essay on Comedy and the Uses of the Comic Spirit* (London: Archibald Constable and Company, 1897): 77.

2   Luke McKernan, review of Frank Gray (ed), *The Hove Pioneers and the Arrival of Cinema*, *Journal of Popular British Cinema* 2 (1999): 144-145.

3   J S Bratton, "Beating the bounds: gender play and role reversal in the Edwardian music hall", in Michael R Booth and Joel H Kaplan (eds), *The Edwardian Theatre: Essays on performance and the stage* (Cambridge: Cambridge University Press, 1996): 96.

4   Max Beerbohm, *Zuleika Dobson* (London: Minerva, 1991 [1911]): 68.

5   The Old Stager, *The Actor's Handbook and Guide to the Stage* (London: Dick's, 1884): 25.

6   Sigmund Freud, *Jokes and their Relation to the Unconscious*, translated and edited by James Strachey (London: Routledge & Kegan Paul, 1960): 185.

7   Translated from the French: "Si franc qu'on le suppose, le rire cache une arrière-pensée d'entente, je dirais presque de complicité, avec d'autres rieurs, réels ou imaginaires". Henri Bergson, *Le Rire: Essai sur la signification du comique* (Paris: Presses Universitaires de France, 1940 [1899]): 5.

A Sequestered "Poodle-faker": Droll, Camp and Ivor Novello

Michael Williams

This essay arises from work-in-progress on the film career of Ivor Novello, and marks an attempt to highlight the funny-peculiar, if not downright queer, side of this star as he appears, standing at the door, in the eponymous and most suspicious role in Alfred Hitchcock's *The Lodger* (1926). I will begin by highlighting the rather disparaging way in which critics have apprehended Novello's work in this film and others, and then proceed by asking whether there might be something more substantive to the queerness of Novello's "camp" than mere histrionics.

The perceived anachronism of the "amusingly odd"

Although it might seem rather obvious, critics of Novello's films routinely foreground the star's *performance* in their writing above all else, or, to be more specific, his performance *style*. Crucially, this style is often named only to be denigrated. In films such as *The Lodger*, certainly his best-known film role as a mysterious stranger who bears a striking resemblance to the murderous figure known as "The Avenger" (who attacks only blonde women), Novello's presence has been generally perceived by modern critics as somewhat eccentric, even anachronistic.

It is as if the Hitchcock film and the Novello film were two separate entities, the former deserving critical acclaim despite the sometimes comical influence of the latter. As Lindsay Anderson put it: "Novello's performance is throughout extremely crude (and often, now, very funny)".[1] Even contemporary critics found on occasion that his acting style sounded a note of apparent disharmony in his pictures, with *Variety* commenting on Novello's performance in Adrian Brunel's 1923 film *The Man Without Desire* that "he is overly 'pretty' and his gestures at times remind one of a highly hysterical girl, but there is no doubt that he will be the picture's great attraction".[2]

The word "camp" could have been on the tip of the tongue of both writers, but is made explicit in a 1976 review of *The Lodger* in the *Monthly Film Bulletin*. The magazine, not surprisingly, celebrates Hitchcock's film as the hallowed cornerstone of the director's career, but deigns to accord only curiosity value to Novello's presence, which it bluntly labels "dated theatrical camp". The unfortunate corollary of this "camp", the article suggests, is that "the tension between Novello's luminous matinée-idol presence and his function as a potential candidate for sex murder all but obliterates the role".[3] This position would seem to concur with that of Hitchcock, who, in his famous interviews with François Truffaut, constantly emphasised only the *difficulty* of constructing the film's narrative around Novello, saying: "Ivor Novello, the leading man, was a matinée idol in England. He was a very big name at the time. These are the problems we face with the star system. Very often the story line is jeopardised because a star cannot be a villain."[4]

If Hitchcock were to be believed, it would seem as if the star's performance, or even mere presence, constitutes some kind of obstacle to the intended meaning of the film, particularly in respect to the idea of guilt. But do we have the makings of a "camp" reading of Novello's film performances here, and how might that relate to the articulation of the notions of guilt and innocence?

"Even if he's a bit queer, he's a gentleman"

When watching *The Lodger* again, in an attempt to quantify the curious mixed appeal of its star in this apparently most unlikely role as a serial killer, my interest was sparked by one of the lines spoken (in an intertitle, of course) by the lodger's landlady, played by Marie Ault. This line arises as the redoubtable Mrs Bunting, who has let a room to Novello, defends her new tenant against the insinuations of cocky policeman Joe (Malcolm Keen), the eager but somewhat inept suitor to young Daisy Bunting (June), who holds the suspicion, strongly corroborated by "evidence" in the film, that the lodger gets up to no good every time he sneaks out into those dark London streets at night. The allegations of Joe, who had previously exclaimed in his relief at the lodger's very strange early disinterest in the same young woman, "Anyway, I'm glad he's not keen on the girls", are silenced by Mrs Bunting when she utters the words: "Don't be silly, Joe, he's not that sort", before continuing: "Even if he's a bit queer, he's a gentleman".

The implication of this innuendo might seem very clear to modern eyes and ears – that Novello's lodger might not be much of a "ladies man", so to speak, particularly given that today Ivor Novello, the luminous idol of romance, is widely known to have been gay. This knowledge activates a sort of retrospective irony when viewing the film, of the kind that Barbara Klinger observes in *Melodrama and Meaning* (1994).[5] Klinger gives the example of Douglas Sirk's *All That Heaven Allows* (1955), which stars Rock Hudson, another matinée idol who was later discovered to be gay. Thus, audiences since the mid-1980s have enjoyed seeing the star quizzed by his co-star, Jane Wyman, who wonders just when he is finally going to get around to finding the right girl, or asks Wyman, "Don't you think you're susceptible?". Klinger suggests that "[t]he droll response that accompanies these moments confirms the fact that camp audiences may be cognizant of the substantial artifice behind romantic conceits and gender roles in the melodrama without necessarily developing such awareness in progressive directions. Mass camp recognition simply translates this 'incongruity' in sexual preference into the ridiculous".[6]

By the term "mass camp", Klinger is referring to that dislocation of camp in the latter half of this century from its gay point of reference, a process which cultural historians such as Moe Meyer[7] largely attribute to Susan Sontag's highly influential 1964 essay, "Notes on 'Camp'", in which she states that camp "is art that proposes itself seriously, but cannot be taken altogether seriously because it is 'too much'".[8] This appears to be the same "dated theatrical camp" that the *Monthly Film Bulletin* found ridiculous in Novello's performance, resulting from the perceived anachronism of the droll, or amusingly odd, where present standards and prejudices gaze with amused disdain at past forms, a gaze that Philip Core terms "a form of historicism viewed histrionically".[9]

Meyer seeks to relocate the substance of this style, arguing that Sontag has neglected what he sees as the original and fundamental function of camp, which is that "[w]hether one subscribes to an essentialist or constructionist theory of gay and lesbian identity, it comes down to the fact that, at some time, the actor must *do* something in order to produce the social visibility by which the identity is manifested. Postures, gestures, costume and dress, and speech acts become the elements that constitute both the identity and the identity performance".[10]

We thus have to ask whether the performance of Novello is merely a droll anachronism, or a gay identity performance?

An etymological diversion

One of the difficulties here is that information about Novello's sexuality, whether manifested on the cinema screen or not, was probably privy only to those "in the know", largely those in film and theatrical circles and that group of gentlemen who embodied the gay 1920s in every sense, including the likes of Noël Coward and Beverley Nichols, whom Hugh David terms "the society homosexual".[11] Thus, perhaps we should not be too eager to read this use of the adjective "queer", which also pervades, to a degree of obsession, the 1913 Marie Belloc Lowndes novel on which the film is based, as a synonym for "gay".[12] Or should we?

I would like to begin answering this question by making a slight etymological diversion. According to H Montgomery Hyde,[13] the word "queer" was certainly in use as a slang term for "homosexual" by the time *The Lodger* was made, and, given the accounts of that film's production by Donald Spoto[14] and Robin Wood,[15] the intimations of these intertitles were unlikely to have escaped the mischievous director's attention.

The word "queer", more so than today, could mean many things and refer to many qualities of "Otherness". The 1913 Webster dictionary suggests that "queer" stems from the Latin "torquere", meaning "to twist", translating through the English "thwart", "through" and – most intriguing of all – "torture".[16] Thus, these definitions already suggest a twisted, tortured figure which stands in direct opposition to the norm, and for which, considering Novello's association with the First World War and his composition of the song "Keep the Home Fires Burning", his role as the haunted stranger in *The Lodger* has many fascinating implications – implications which are unfortunately beyond the scope of this essay. The dictionary goes on to describe one that is "at variance with what is usual and normal", but who is furthermore "mysterious; suspicious; questionable". The queerness of Novello's "lodger" is perhaps becoming apparent.

The British Empire Universities Modern English Illustrated Dictionary of 1924 adds a note of humour to this figure when it cites "droll" as an interchangeable synonym for "queer" in the sense of an odd type of humour that verges on the playful burlesque or parody.[17] We might call this a sense of knowing articulation, a certain recognition of gestures of hidden knowledge, "droll" being that dry type of humour that can only be articulated through an unconvincingly *straight*-faced manner, and which always takes a few moments for its true significance to be realised. In this usage, droll comes very close to camp, although the latter must be more exaggerated and blatant: dry vs. wet senses of humour, perhaps.

For possible evidence of a camp reading of Novello in the 1920s, however, we must look to *The New York Times*, as it indicates that it was not particularly enthralled by *The Lodger*, or *The Case of Jonathan Drew* as it was known in the United States. In a delightfully acerbic 1928 review entitled "Novello in Lurid film", the emphasis is once more placed upon the star who "rents a room from the parents of a light-haired girl, locks his travelling bag in the closet and settles down for a period of over-acting". The most apposite observation, however, is made as the review describes Novello's first appearance in the film, as Mrs Bunting opens the door to this fog-enshrouded figure, who looks for all the world like an inverted exclamation mark: "There now enters Mr. Novello, looking pale and drawn and with a manner plainly saying that he very likely doesn't care for blondes at all".[18]

An implicit, even explicit, link is being made in that delicate phrase "a manner plainly saying" between an excessively expressive, mannered form of camp, and a likely indifference to "blondes" and, by implication, women *per se*. This kind of euphemistic slippage is perhaps also evident in the title of Novello's 1923 film, *The Man Without Desire*, directed by Adrian Brunel. In Brunel's film, the star plays a man who awakens from a centuries-old slumber to discover that he is impotent. Knowing that Novello is the star suggests an alternative title – "The Man Without Desire (For Women)".

While *The New York Times* review is important in indicating that Novello's performance style in the 1920s could be read as camp, and moreover, camp as gay, it is equally important to recognise that the "queerness" of Novello is much more than just a vague inference of homosexuality, even if that does provide the crucial starting-point of this persona. Equally, one would hesitate to suggest that there is any correlation between camp and just plain bad acting (although some might disagree).

"To think that dolled-up poodle-faker was once one of us!"

I suggest that, in *The Lodger*, Novello's camp persona functions to register a kind of surrogate ulterior motive, where the star's camp articulation of difference or Otherness along ambiguously sexual lines serves to add symbolic evidence that the lodger and the mysterious avenger are one and the same.

There are several moments in Hitchcock's film when such hermeneutic slippage becomes apparent, not least at the climax of the sequence that inspired *The New York Times*' remark, where the camp Novello, having ensconced himself in his new room, communicates great distress on finding himself surrounded by quaint Victorian prints of nude and semi-nude women hanging on the walls. In this scene, Novello's gaze at the female form could scarcely be further removed from desire, as Hitchcock carefully matches a point-of-view shot (from Novello's perspective) as the camera pans across the pictures from right to left, while punctuating the sequence with reaction shots of the lodger's mortified expressions. As if to compound the impression that the matinée idol is unwilling or unable to reciprocate entreaties of female desire, a later sequence set in a fashion house finds Novello thwarting such overtures of romance.

Immediately after a short scene set in the Bunting's kitchen, in which their suspicions of their lodger are made clear, the film cuts to a medium close-up on Novello, who gazes rather solemnly at the fashion parade before which he is seated, while a wider shot indicates that he is flanked by two women. Soon, the woman seated on the left of the screen leans towards Novello, who is holding a cigarette limply in his right hand, and then adjusts her dress in the manner of a flirtation. No response. Then the woman seated to his right taps a cigarette from its case, then holds it in her mouth as she searches for a light, before she can find it, Novello reaches out to afford her a light from his own lighter, as we cut to a mid-shot that highlights the fact that the lodger never once looks at her, his eyes unblinkingly staring ahead. At the end of the sequence, as Novello leaves, the woman on the right makes a resigning gesture with her arm as if to say "drat!".

While, on one level, Novello's disinterest in the two women at the fashion house could be attributed to his single-minded (but rather ambiguous) affection for Daisy, who models at the establishment, it remains one moment of many in which the extratextual sexuality of Novello is obliquely signified through an onscreen characterisation – a disjuncture between being, quite literally, surrounded by

104

women, whether in art or life, and being the object of heterosexual desire, while nevertheless articulating that he is not quite of this inclination.

However, such symbolic juxtaposition is perhaps most apparent in the figure of *The Rat* (1925), in which Novello plays the eponymous role of a roguish Apache of the Parisian underworld, and appears to be having a great deal of fun playing the role that he once described as "a curious blending of a child, angel and devil".[19] In this film, as in *The Lodger*, Novello makes a great entrance. After being pursued (for some unknown misdemeanour) by two members of the local gendarmerie, "The Rat" arrives at the apartment where his friend Odile (Mae Marsh) awaits him. As Novello climbs the dark stairway, performance is again the byword as the star verily skips up the steps cigarette in hand, before hastily brushing himself down, adjusting his apparel, and calling to Odile inside. The closed door designates an important frame of transformation in the scene, for it is over this threshold that Novello effects, in a matter of seconds, the remarkable transition between what can be described as a mince, to the posturing swagger that he so enjoys once he has entered the apartment, thus beautifully demonstrating the camp double emphasis on his performance. He even attaches his Apache cap to the wall by throwing his trusty blade at it, just to crown this excessive display of masculinity which, one might say, has all the subtlety of bullfighting. This seems a parody – a drollery of a queer masculinity (in every sense). One might say that Novello's "Rat" protests his heterosexuality too much, rather like his counterpart in America, Rudolph Valentino, who regularly posed for publicity shots with cars and muscle-building weights, or acted as a judge in beauty pageants in an attempt to "prove" his masculinity and heterosexuality and thereby undermine the constant media speculation about his sexuality. This speculation culminated in the infamous "Pink Powder Puffs" article of *The Chicago Tribune* that attempted to link the "effeminacy" of Valentino in his films with an implicit homosexuality and perceived decline in the machismo of the American male.[20]

Interestingly, in *The Triumph of the Rat* (1926), the first sequel to *The Rat*, which received trade show screenings in the same month, September, as *The Lodger*, and only two months after the powder-puffs article, a group of underworld denizens are seen to pore over a copy of a society magazine, a close-up of which reveals a photograph of Novello surrounded by eight adoring women. The patrons are incredulous of the excessive image, one of them exclaiming the rather classic line: "To think that dolled-up poodle-faker was once one of us!". A "poodle-faker" was a young man who "makes a point of socializing with women",[21] which could mean many things, but is perhaps more suggestive of a lapdog than a ladies' man. The term seems perfectly suited to a star so strongly associated with a perceived appeal to women, but who never quite manages to love them back in the way expected.

In conclusion, the transposition of the distrust of such appearances, and particularly grand entrances, to *The Lodger* leaves us with a highly suspicious individual. Rather than being a dated anachronism or the bland epitome of innocence that Hitchcock complained about, the function, I suggest, of the camp flip side of Novello perceived by *The New York Times*, with that "pale and drawn" countenance, is that it is highly conducive to suspicion, carrying that burden of guilt associated with something repressed or concealed. In this sense, any tension or conflict aroused in the film by Novello as an "incongruous" matinée idol is wholly positive; indeed, such symbolic tensions fuel the heart of Novello's star persona. In this respect, Novello's presence is essential to the production of meaning in *The Lodger*, a film that derives its narrative energy from the imaginative disjuncture between what is seen and what is suspected. Here, every incriminating angle, decoy, suspicion and exaggerated manner are not merely the consequence of dated style or celluloid anachronism, they are decidedly queer glimpses, in every sense, of the sequestered identities of Ivor Novello.

Notes

[1]   Quoted in Geoffrey Macnab, "Looking for Lustre: Stars at Gainsborough", in Pam Cook (ed), *Gainsborough Pictures* (London; Washington: Cassell, 1997): 103.

[2]   *Variety* 12 March 1924.

[3]   Richard Combs, "Lodger: A Story of the London Fog, The", *Monthly Film Bulletin* 43: 510 (July 1976): 156.

[4]   François Truffaut, *Hitchcock* (London; Toronto; Sydney; New York: Paladin, 1978): 48.

[5]   Barbara Klinger, *Melodrama and Meaning: History, Culture, and the Films of Douglas Sirk* (Bloomington; Indianapolis: Indiana University Press, 1994).

[6]   Ibid: 151.

[7]   Moe Meyer (ed), *The Politics and Poetics of Camp* (London; New York: Routledge, 1994).

[8]   Susan Sontag, "Notes on 'Camp'", in *Against Interpretation and Other Essays* (New York; London; Toronto; Sydney; Auckland: Anchor Books/Doubleday, 1990): 284.

[9]   Philip Core, *Camp: The Lie That Tells the Truth* (New York: Delilah Books, 1984): 7, quoted in Klinger: 132.

[10]   Meyer: 4. Emphasis in original.

[11]   Hugh David, *On Queer Street: A Social History of British Homosexuality 1895-1995* (London: Harper Collins, 1997): 79.

[12]   Marie Belloc Lowndes, *The Lodger* (Chicago: Academy, 1988) [first published in 1913].

[13]   H Montgomery Hyde, *The Other Love: An Historical and Contemporary Survey of Homosexuality in Britain* (London: Heinemann, 1970): 22.

[14]   Donald Spoto, *The Life of Alfred Hitchcock: The Dark Side of Genius* (London: Collins, 1983).

[15]   Robin Wood, *Hitchcock's Films Revisited* (New York: Columbia University Press, 1989).

[16]   Definition of "queer" retrieved from the online *ARTFL Project: Webster Dictionary, 1913* (http://machaut.uchicago.edu/cgi-bin/WEBSTER.WORD=queer), retrieved over the Internet, 11 February 1998.

[17]   Edward D Price (ed), *The British Empire Universities Modern English Illustrated Dictionary* (London: The Syndicate Publishing Company, 1924).

[18]   "Novello in Lurid Film", *The New York Times* 11 June 1928: 27: 1.

[19]   Quotation taken from the final instalment of a nine-part series, attributed to the authorship of Novello himself: "Life Romance of Ivor Novello: Composer, Stage and Screen Star", *Picture Show* 13: 318 (30 May 1925): 18.

[20]   "Pink Powder Puffs", *The Chicago Tribune* 19 July 1926: 10.

[21]   *Collins English Dictionary* (London: Harper Collins, 1995).

Hitchcock the Joker

Robert Murphy

Mordant humour seeps into all of Hitchcock's films. Of his ten silent films, two – *The Farmer's Wife* and *Champagne* (both 1927) – count as comedies, but humour intrudes even in his most serious films.[1] One of the remarkable things about Hitchcock is how early he develops a distinctive view of the world which combines an interest in the bizarre with a mischievous and dark sense of humour. He holds together a realist's interest in everyday life with an Expressionist concern with how a banal surface can be scraped away to reveal the strange and fantastic reality beneath. The result is a world-view which is disturbing, but leavened by humour.

Behind the image of flappers and Bright Young Things, the 1920s were a sombre decade, with European society reeling from the effects of the war. As Donald Spoto explains:

> The war of 1914-1918 brought the ultimate challenge to nineteenth-century absolutes and transformed the social and economic structure of Great Britain. The world had literally exploded in violence and death, and these realities filled everyone's consciousness daily. Psychological stress, the transient nature of this world, the precarious order of civilization, the sudden eruption of madness in local crimes – these burst in on a world of rapidly advancing technology at the same time as the most dramatic means of entertainment was reaching millions weekly.[2]

Film is an invaluable guide to these emotional events, and Expressionism, which as a movement captured the unease and disruption of the period, is crucial in providing a means for exploring them.

Classic German Expressionist films such as *Das Kabinett des Dr Caligari* (*The Cabinet of Doctor Caligari*, 1919) and *Nosferatu* (1921) are gloomy and disturbing, and one might expect Hitchcock's most Expressionist-influenced films – *The Pleasure Garden* (1926), *The Lodger* (1926) and *Blackmail* (1929) – to share their ethos. Their stories, although they lack a supernatural element, are certainly morbid. In *The Pleasure Garden*, Patsy (Virginia Valli), a world-weary but good-hearted chorus girl, befriends an ingénue, Jill (Carmelita Geraghty), rescuing her from lecherous stage-door Johnnies, sharing her bed and board with her, and getting her a job in the chorus line. But this pseudo-innocent proves to be ruthless, exploitative and ambitious, and she is quickly promoted to a starring role. She dumps her friend Patsy who, on the rebound (there is a lesbian subtext), marries a man who turns out to be an adulterer and a murderer.

In *The Lodger*, a showgirl, Daisy (June Tripp), strikes up a romance with

107

her family's lodger (Ivor Novello) whom we have every reason to believe is the Ripper-like character responsible for murdering blonde young women in the London fog. Actually, he is a rich and respectable gentleman trying to find the killer himself and avenge the murder of his sister. Thus, Daisy is vindicated in preferring this potentially dangerous stranger to her dull policeman fiancé, in choosing the exotic over the everyday. For much of the film, however, she appears to be risking her life in the pursuit of wealth and glamour.

In *Blackmail*, Alice (Anny Ondra) engineers a tiff with her boyfriend (another policeman) so that she can flirt with a more interesting-looking chap who tells her that he is an artist. He entices her back to his studio, and, when he tries to rape her, she stabs him to death. A petty criminal guesses that she has killed him, and tries to blackmail her. But he is intimidated by the policeman boyfriend and chased to his death. Alice's temptation away from bourgeois respectability leads to attempted rape, blackmail and two deaths. She is saved, but trapped forever in the guilty secret which she shares with the policeman who will become her husband.

These films are much darker than Hitchcock's most popular British films, *The 39 Steps* (1935) and *The Lady Vanishes* (1938), which are essentially comedy thrillers, but they do have comic elements, and the way in which humour finds its way into these tales of intrigue, betrayal and murder is revealing of Hitchcock's sensibility.

Comedy comes in most obviously and most originally through visual gags. One could cite the Siamese twins at the wedding in *The Ring* (1927), one of whom wants to sit on one side, with the bride's party, and one on the other, with the groom's. But this sort of joke – which has no narrative function – is less typical than the scenes in which Hitchcock uses humour to move the story forward. In *The Pleasure Garden*, we already have suspicions about Jill because Patsy's dog does not like her. But it is the scene in which she kneels down to say her prayers and the dog annoys her by licking the soles of her feet which fully exposes her as a hypocrite. In *Easy Virtue* (1927), the most inventive sequence in this stage-bound melodrama is where the switchboard-operator (Benita Hume) listens in on a late-night telephone conversation between the glamorous divorcee (Isabel Jeans) and her young admirer (Robin Irvine), and we see in her facial expressions the progress of his marriage proposal to her. In *Downhill* (1927), Ivor Novello, as a disgraced public schoolboy disowned by his family, is courting – with little chance of success – a very worldly actress (Isabel Jeans) who appears to be already involved in a relationship with a more mature man (Ian Hunter). Unexpectedly, he inherits £30 000 from a kindly aunt (big money in 1927), and the actress becomes much more interested. But what about the other man who might well be her lover? We do not see him when Novello is telling her the big news – we just become aware of pipe smoke curling up over the back of an armchair. But this is enough to make us realise that these two are partners, and that the schoolboy is going to be fleeced of his money. This works as a sort of Eisensteinian metaphor – the pipe is the man – but it is also surreally funny.

Hitchcock relies much less on dialogue: where witty title cards appear, they often elucidate what is happening visually. In *The Pleasure Garden*, an elderly admirer tells Patsy that "I've fallen in love with that charming kiss curl of yours", to which she replies: "Then I hope you'll be very happy together". But the humour comes less from the dialogue than from the fact that we see Patsy remove her hairpiece (incidentally revealing herself as much less fluffy) and give it to her admirer.

Dialogue dates easily, and serious lines can now seem risible. In *Downhill*, Novello's plea to the headmaster on being expelled for getting the waitress from Ye

Olde Bunne Shoppe pregnant, "Can I – won't I be able to play for the Old Boys, Sir?", now appears ludicrous. At the end of *Easy Virtue,* Isabel Jeans goes out to face the reporters' cameras after her second divorce to make the histrionic declaration, "Shoot, there's nothing left to kill!", which Hitchcock confessed to Truffaut was the "worst title" he had ever written.[3] Where dialogue adds intentional humour, it tends to grow out of character. Fully-fledged comic characters do not emerge in Hitchcock's films until the appearance of Gordon Harker in *The Ring,* where he is supplemented by a cast of fairground freaks, and in *The Farmer's Wife,* where he is supported by a range of rural eccentrics. From *The Pleasure Garden* onwards, however, Hitchcock's interest in the quirks and foibles of everyday behaviour leads him to add comic touches to minor characters such as Patsy's landlady and her husband. Similar comic touches enliven the scenes of Daisy's home life in *The Lodger,* and find full expression in the sound version of *Blackmail* with the gossipy customer who thinks killing someone with a knife is so despicably un-English.

Even at school, Hitchcock played practical jokes, and his activities at Elstree and Lime Grove Studios are notorious.[4] Thus, it is illuminating to compare the humour of his practical joking with that in his films. His jokes can be put loosely into three categories. Firstly, there are those primarily motivated by curiosity: the dinner party he organised for Gertrude Lawrence where the guests were confronted with blue soup, blue trout, blue peaches and blue ice cream, for example.[5] Secondly, there are those where curiosity is mingled with a sadistic desire to discomfort and disturb, such as when Sir Gerald Du Maurier turned up in greasepaint and a kilt to what Hitchcock had led him to believe was a fancy dress party, only to find the other guests dressed formally for a black-tie supper.[6] Thirdly, there were those expressly designed to humiliate and embarrass, from his childlike habit of getting people to sit on farting cushions, to the machiavellian plot which Spoto relates about a crew member inveigled into spending the night chained to a camera in a deserted studio. Hitchcock proffered him laxative-laced brandy to help him through the night, with the consequence that his internal organs, rather than the studio ghost, made the experience an ordeal and left him humiliated and degraded in the morning.

Humour in the films can be similarly graded, from the relative innocuousness of Patsy removing her kiss curls, to Daisy's boyfriend playfully handcuffing her, to the macabre sequence in *The Pleasure Garden* in which the native girl (Nita Naldi) looks thankfully at her lover (Patsy's husband) wading into the sea to rescue her when, in fact, he is coming to hold her head under the waves and make sure that she drowns. This is hardly funny, but the reversal of expectations gives a comic jolt.

Truffaut, arguing against Charles Higham's description of Hitchcock as a "practical joker, a cunning and sophisticated cynic", asserts that Hitchcock's cynicism is "the façade that serves to conceal his pessimism".[7] One might argue the same about his humour, but the element of jokiness betrays a playfulness which reaches beyond both cynicism and pessimism. Comedy is effective in Hitchcock's films because he uses it as a way of making sense of the world. Whereas Hitchcock's practical jokes were often cruel and vulgar, the humour in his films is aestheticised: it adds pathos, offers insight into character, and makes the films richer and more significant. Hitchcock's personal flaws and weaknesses become strengths in his films.

Notes

1   The first five films were made for Michael Balcon's company, Gainsborough (*The Pleasure Garden, The Mountain Eagle, The Lodger, Downhill* and *Easy Virtue*), the last five (*The Ring, The Farmer's Wife, Champagne, The Manxsman* and *Blackmail*) for John Maxwell's company, British International Pictures. Sound and silent versions of *Blackmail* were made; for a comparison of the two versions, see Charles Barr, "Blackmail: Silent & Sound", *Sight and Sound* 52: 2 (spring 1983): 123-126.

2   Donald Spoto, *The Life of Alfred Hitchcock: The Dark Side of Genius* (London: Collins, 1983): 89-90.

3   François Truffaut, *Hitchcock* (London; Toronto; Sydney; New York: Paladin, 1978): 58.

4   "It started with "fly-ripping" (ripping open fly buttons) while the victim was engaged in carrying props or swinging a sound boom, and went on to such items as "windmill-blowing wagers which could leave the unsuspecting winner to saunter around the studios with lamp-blackened face". Patricia Warren, *Elstree Studios* (London: Elm Tree Books, 1984): 49-51; see also Spoto: 109-112, and Michael Balcon, *Michael Balcon presents... A Lifetime of Films* (London: Hutchinson, 1969): 82.

5   Spoto: 110.

6   Ibid: 111.

7   Truffaut: 25.

News from the Archives: Silent Material Held in the British Pathé News Archive

Jenny Hammerton

There are many silent treasures in the vaults of British Pathé News. The Archive takes care of an estimated 55 000 000' of film, with most of its holdings on original 35mm nitrate. Some of the collection is very well catalogued, while other films are known only by their titles. The database, like many others for holdings of this size, leaves much to be desired.

Luckily, there are moves afoot to recatalogue the collection and make it more accessible to researchers and programme-makers. Every film in the *Eve Pic* collection (approximately 2400 silent cinemagazine items) has been viewed and described in detail, and the early documentaries are next. The work is time-consuming, but has proved extremely rewarding. Much is being learned about this remarkable holding of news and social history film.

The majority of films have accompanying paperwork. For the silent material, this may be just an "issue sheet" which lists each of the stories in a particular reel by title and one-line summary. Some collections have longer shotlists and information about the source of footage.

Pathé's silent material can be divided up as follows:

☐ *Pathé Gazette* (1910-29). Some items have decomposed, but the collection is in fairly good shape overall. Issue sheets listing details of each story are available for most of this material.

☐ *Pathé Pictorial* (1917-31). Material from the 1920s and early 1930s which survives has been fully described. It is currently not possible to ascertain how much of the earlier material still exists. The *Pictorial* was Pathé's main cinemagazine (featuring sports, work, hobbies, and so on), and continued in various incarnations to 1969.

☐ *Eve's Film Review* (1921-33). All items which survive have been fully described. This cinemagazine for women, features fashion, beauty regimes, women's sports and home crafts. There are also regular glimpses of theatrical performers and cabaret entertainers of the period.

☐ *UN*. This is the "Unused" or "Unissued" collection, and incorporates foreign stories bought in for reuse, stock shots and some out-takes. Pathé exchanged many of its stories with other branches of the company around the world, and also bought-in material from freelance filmmakers.

☐ *ON*. The *Old Negatives* is a collection of 1890s and early 1900s material. This is mostly early *Pathé Gazette* stories, but there are also some bought-in comedy films and stock shots.

☐ *Documentaries.* This collection includes educational material by British Instructional Films and sponsored documentaries such as those for Morris Cars and Heinz.

The Pathé database is searchable on the Internet at the following address: www.britishpathe.com. The database can be somewhat problematic. Due to data-inputting errors many years ago, there are incorrect reference numbers, spelling mistakes, duplications and omissions. These are currently being corrected.

The database descriptions for the Pathé News collections have been written with television researchers in mind. The resource is used mainly by Pathé staff researching film available either for programme-makers, or for in-house productions. Researchers are welcome to consult the computer database in our London office which allows for more complex searches. Attendance in person has an added advantage in that the researcher is also able to consult Pathé's card index. This is the research tool of preference for some, and can often throw up some interesting links to other material. Unfortunately, the card index is not complete. Unscrupulous researchers may have misfiled cards or even (it is rumoured) taken cards home and not returned them! In-depth research is best served by a combination of the two mediums.

There is also the magic ingredient – the brains of the Pathé staff. The Chief Librarian has been with the company since he was a post boy, and has an encyclopedic knowledge of the material, as do other members of the research staff; the technical staff have seen millions of hours of footage pass before their eyes and have photographic memories. If clients are having difficulty finding the images they need, a casual query can sometimes spark off an inspirational train of thought leading to gems of unexpected material.

The silent material is stored in purpose-built nitrate vaults at Pinewood Studios. The material is in surprisingly good condition, and some of the film has been little used. Occasionally, tinted and toned material is discovered which looks incredibly fresh, as it probably has not been across sprockets since the 1920s. An ongoing preservation programme, printing material onto safety stock until another medium is decided upon, is currently in place.

Although the Archive's main users are commercial programme-makers, bona fide academic researchers are welcome and supported. Broadcasters should contact Larry McKinna or Paul Gost in the London office on +44 171 323 0407. Academic researchers should contact Jenny Hammerton at the Pinewood Studios office on +44 1753 630361.

Index

Notes on contributors

Barry Anthony has written extensively on many areas of Victorian and Edwardian popular culture. He is author of *The Kinora: motion pictures for the home 1896-1914* (1996) and co-author (with Richard Brown) of *A Victorian Film Enterprise: The History of the British Mutoscope and Biograph Company, 1897-1915* (Flicks Books, 1999). He is currently working on a study of early British film comedy, also to be published by Flicks Books.

Alan Burton teaches Media Studies at De Montfort University in Leicester. He has contributed to *Film History* and the *Journal of Popular British Cinema*, and co-edited two studies of British filmmakers: *Liberal Directions: Basil Dearden and Postwar British Film Culture* (Flicks Books, 1997) and *The Family Way: The Boulting Brothers and British Film Culture* (Flicks Books, 2000).

Ann-Marie Cook is an Adjunct Professor of Film Studies at the University of the Pacific, Stockton, California, and is completing a PhD thesis, which deals with the political implications of the contemporary British heritage film, at the University of East Anglia.

Bryony Dixon has worked at the British Film Institute for the past eight years, supplying access to the NFTVA's viewing collection for research and theatrical screenings in the UK and internationally.

Tony Fletcher is a founder member of The Cinema Museum in London, and is currently researching a companies' history of British silent fiction cinema. In the 1980s, he made two short films, including one on the actress Renée Adorée.

Christine Gledhill is Professor of Cinema Studies at Staffordshire University. She has written widely on feminist film theory, melodrama and British cinema. She is currently preparing *Reframing Cinema: 1918-1928*, to be published in 2001.

Frank Gray is Curator of the South East Film and Video Archive at the University of Brighton. His research is devoted to George Albert Smith, James Williamson and the beginnings of cinema in Sussex.

Jenny Hammerton is a graduate of the University of East Anglia's MA in Film Archiving course. She is Pathé's Senior Cataloguer and coordinates their recataloguing programme. She is particularly interested in silent non-narrative film, and is currently researching fashion presentation in the newsreel.

Michael Hammond lectures in Film Studies in the English Department at the University of Southampton. He is presently completing his PhD thesis entitled "The Big Show: British Cinema Culture in the Great War".

Luke McKernan has written and lectured on various aspects of British cinema history, and is currently researching the life of documentary producer Charles Urban. He is Head of Information at the British Universities Film and Video Council.

Judith McLaren is a teacher at St Paul's School in London, and a part-time MA student at the University of Westminster.

Garrett Monaghan is Senior Lecturer in Media Art and the Moving Image at the University of Portsmouth. His research focuses on the reception of the early moving image, and on the use of the moving image as a medium for autobiographical practices.

Robert Murphy is author of *Realism and Tinsel* (1989) and *Sixties British Cinema* (1992), and editor of *The British Cinema Book* (1997) and *British Cinema of the 90s* (2000). He is Senior Research Fellow at De Montfort University.

Laraine Porter is Director of the Broadway Media Centre in Nottingham. She is Coordinator of the British Silent Cinema Weekend, and has published on women and comedy in *Because I Tell a Joke or Two* (1998).

Amy Sargeant lectures in Film and Media Art. She has previously published on silent British cinema in *Moving Performance: British Stage and Screen, 1890s-1920s* (Flicks Books, 2000), *Visual Delights: Essays on the Popular and Projected Image in the 19th Century* (Flicks Books, 2000) and *Film Studies*. She is currently writing on architecture and early cinema.

Frank Scheide teaches Film History and Criticism at the University of Arkansas in Fayetteville. He is currently writing a book on the influence of the music-hall on Chaplin's early film career, and cataloguing the British Film Institute's collection of Chaplin out-takes from 1917 to 1946.

Jamie Sexton is a research student at the University of East Anglia, where he has also taught. He is currently completing a PhD on avant-garde and alternative film culture in interwar Britain.

Trish Sheils is currently Film Education Officer for the Cambridge Film Consortium based at the Arts Picturehouse in Cambridge. Her postgraduate studies include an MA in Theatre and Film at Sheffield University, and an MPhil on the postwar melodramatic films of Powell and Pressburger. Her current interest is the links between silent cinema and 19th-century theatre.

Gerry Turvey teaches Sociology at Kingston University. He is currently researching the history of the British and Colonial Kinematograph Company, and investigating Ivor Montagu's contribution to British film culture.

Michael Williams is currently researching a PhD on the film career of Ivor Novello at the University of East Anglia.